HIGHWAY
TO HEAVEN

HIGHWAY
TO HEAVEN

HARRY BLAMIRES

Thomas Nelson Publishers
Nashville • Camden • New York

To
Bernard Markham

Nostrum est interim
mentem erigere
et totis patriam
votis appetere.

ABELARD

Foreword to edition of 1984

A "Divine Trilogy" can be completed only by a glimpse of Heaven. But the narrator's pilgrimage cannot take him right inside Heaven or we shall never hear his story. He has to be content with a journey across the Borderlands. That of course is a more cheerful experience than visiting Hell's borderlands or Hell itself. Certainly I enjoyed writing *Highway to Heaven* (originally called *Blessing Unbounded*) more than any other book I have written. If I have a personal favourite among my theological books it is this. After all, there is bound to be a flavour of sourness about satire that consigns human characters to Hell. Satire which makes fun of people who are on their way to Heaven can be entirely free of such sourness. In those who stray from the highway and think they can run a better show on their own outside the walls of God's city, one can satirise foolishness and wilfulness, but the prevailing atmosphere, so near to Heaven, scarcely allows of harshness.

We do not expect to find here grosser forms of self-centredness and worldliness, for the practitioners of such idolatries have all gone elsewhere. Nevertheless, there is ample opportunity to poke fun at the variety of forms in which we Christians choose to worship and the diversity of our emphases in doctrine. This has to be done without questioning that very dissimilar Christian bodies may indeed be heavenwardbound, and hence there is a current of ecumenical sympathy in this book which may prove congenial to the 1980s.

The prevailing good-humour of the story ensured that those who reviewed the book for the most part treated it kindly and warmly. It provoked them to head their reviews with such light-hearted titles as "Tourist in Heaven", "Marching to Zion", "The Heavenly Hiker", and "One Foot on Earth", and generally they liked it the best of the three. "The writing is swifter and tauter than in the previous volumes, the humour lighter, and the allegory perhaps more convincing," *British Book News* declared.

Below all the fun the book investigates at a serious level such themes as the nature of penitence, the mystery of faith, and the primacy of will over desire that constitutes human freedom ("You will know what you truly wanted only when you have chosen it").

1

Suddenly my dizziness left me and the mists cleared. There was a straight road before me, compelling and decisive, and I knew it was the way to Heaven. How I knew this I cannot say, since from all appearances it might almost have been the road to Kettlewell. It was a country of upland pasture, dotted with windswept firs and oaks. In the distance, on either side, the grassland melted into moorland, which in turn sloped up to a wall of white crags. I was conscious of being on the heights, in a wide pass through mountainous country. The great rocky ridges in the distance, which ran parallel to my road, compelled me forward as surely as the road itself. Indeed, as the clouds swept over them, it was easy to fancy that the ridges themselves were in motion at my side. This fancy was encouraged by the very shape of the level limestone barrier on my right, which lay above the billowing pasture and moorland like a giant liner on the waves. Something that looked like a misshapen cairn rose from it above the skyline, giving the appearance of a sloping funnel. The fabric of Nature seemed to be moving forward, like myself, to its everlasting home.

Roads like this invite the stride, not the saunter, and I swung forward zestfully, relieved to feel that my limbs were once more at my own disposal. I cannot say that I had any distinct aim. In pursuing roads of this kind it is sufficient to look forward to the view beyond the next rise; and the track ahead of me rose and fell for as far as the eye could see, at each rise apparently reaching a higher eminence than before.

It would be meaningless to try to suggest for how long I strode forward, mounting one rise after another, but my mood gradually changed. For one thing, I did not seem to make much progress, at least in relation to the ridges stretching out on either side. Perhaps they really *were* moving. I fixed each one alternately with my eyes in a competitive spirit, and was slightly irritated to be assured that their vastness and my comparative slowness explained the fanciful delusion away. The sense of getting nowhere was being exaggerated by my solitariness: so too was the feeling of aimlessness. There was no inn to look forward to, where I could rest, drink a pint of beer and eat some sandwiches. In any case, I had no sandwiches with me. Worse still, I did not feel hungry, or thirsty, or tired; not even mildly so. It was disappointing not to be wanting the little indulgences which brighten a country walk. I found myself, rather absurdly, wishing that I wanted something.

That was how it all began. I invented a need and thought myself into it. I'm lonely, I said: I need companionship. And the more I thought about it, the lonelier I felt.

"Oh, God," I prayed, "leave me not alone!"

When I opened my eyes again, a figure had appeared on the summit of the road ahead, walking towards me. It was a girl.

For a moment or two I studied the characteristics of the approaching figure—the slender, upright build, the graceful shoulders—but I soon stopped, for one does not catalogue a familiar acquaintance, and I knew that I knew her. Instead I began to wonder how I should address her. What degree of familiarity, what degree of reserve, would she expect of me? Could I be quite certain that she would even recognise me? No doubt I had changed in twenty years while she, to my strained eyes, was still a girl. Moreover, to be honest, I was a little uncomfortable because I realised that she would have the advantage over me here. Probably by now she was a resident of some standing in the place.

When she was close enough to greet me, she smiled. And when we came face to face, she held out both her arms in a gesture which invited the arms-length clasping of hands. Rather a stagey greeting, I thought, but at least she's not going to be standoffish.

"Annot," I said. And straightaway my tongue was on the fringe of some stupidly conventional opening such as—You don't look a day older. But it was forestalled, consciously, I'm sure.

"I was sent to you," she said simply.

Certainly she had the advantage. I looked down at my feet.

"I'm glad," I said. "I wanted someone."

"You prayed for someone. And here all prayers are answered at once and quite plainly. You'd better remember that."

From her first words I suspected that she had come to take charge of me, and I did not quite like the idea.

For I flattered myself that formerly I had managed
Annot in a rather accomplished way. Of course I was
only a boy in those days, though with some years' lead
over her. Taking heart from past memories, I tried to
bolster myself with flippancy.

"So you've come to show me the ropes?"

"I've come because you prayed for a friend."

I took courage and stared at her. The same brown
eyes, warm and generous, but purged of that pleading
intensity which had once made me feel so masterful.
The same slight eyebrows, neat and delicate, perhaps
her most distinctive feature, for the full curve of black
eyebrows over eyes like that would have swept the face
with voluptuousness.

"I must admit," I said, "that for an answer to prayer
this is a pretty promising beginning."

Indeed I felt inclined to revise my notions of Heaven
on lines more familiar to Mohammedans. For it had
not previously occurred to me that, in escaping
earthly life, I might be freed from its more irksome social restraints in this delightful way. To be offered the
company of my youth's sweetheart on a lonely highland lane, where all was warmth and beauty, was
something I had never dared to hope for.

"I suppose I shall have to let you lead the way as
usual," I said.

She shook her head.

"It's useless to pretend that we are other than we
are."

"You mean," I said with ironic gallantry, "that I'm
now twenty years older than you and must conduct
myself accordingly."

"No. There is no such difference of age. There never
can be."

"That's comforting," I said. "Then we can walk as we used to do."

I drew her arm through mine, keeping my hand on hers, and we walked on.

"This is what we were when we last saw each other," I said. "A boy and girl falling in love."

"Falling out of love," she corrected.

"We can forget that."

"Now you are a married man."

"I *was*," I said, "but since my wife is now enjoying the advantages of widowhood, it seems scarcely just to press the point."

"I got as far as being engaged myself."

"Yes. I heard about that at the same time as I heard of your smash-up. It seemed terribly tragic at the time."

"It was, for some people."

I wondered for a moment whether there might be a sting in this; but Annot had no cause to play the role of the jilted innocent. We had parted by mutual consent—or at least by mutual neglect of each other.

"It was strange," I said, ruminating on the odd inconclusiveness of our youthful relationship. "Of course, it was only to be expected that you'd find someone else. If you don't mind my saying so, you were not the kind of girl to be left as a wallflower. I don't know the young man, by the way. Is he here?"

"Not yet."

"Then you must make the best of things with me, until he turns up," I said, not at all dissatisfied with the news.

"Your gallantry began as fun. Don't let it develop into serious possessiveness. I've not been sent to you so that you can renew the evil that was between us, but so that you can recapture the good. Certainly there was good. You saw something in me which it is right for you to see again. Otherwise I shouldn't be here."

Was I being seriously possessive? I wasn't quite sure. I only knew that I did not want to be lectured by Annot. I was ready to seize on any device to bluff myself out of the role of her ward.

"My dear," I said, "you really mustn't do this stained-glass window stuff. You don't look the part. If you'd been sent to me clothed in light, and preceded by an angel train, with a warning notice *Do not touch*, I might have found you less irresistible. As it is, you're far too cosy and approachable. At least you might have put on your halo. It would have been some protection. Where is it, by the way? Is it in your handbag?"

Annot remained silent. In a kind of desperation I strove to keep up the banter, for I hated the possibility that she might resume the role of instructress.

"You were quite right to leave it off. I always preferred to see you hatless."

Without a word she ended the banter by turning her face towards me. I saw again, for the first time since our meeting, that searching in her eyes which once I should have called "pleading." But it was a different searching, keen with sympathy yet empty of desire. She did not need to plead with me now. Perhaps because she was pleading for me. The very thought swept me into a flood of recollections.

"Annot, do you remember the first spring walk we had together? You remember picnicking by the river at Appletreewick, tea in the little cottage at Bolton Abbey, and then the long evening trek over Beamsley Beacon in the pouring rain?"

She squeezed my arm.

"We didn't much mind the rain," she said. "We had to share one mackintosh: that made it bearable."

"It's odd," I said, "but before you came along I was thinking how like Wharfedale this is."

"It is. It's meant to be. But it won't last for long."

She pointed to the top of the rise we were climbing. And a few moments later, just before we reached the summit, she stopped me.

"Close your eyes for two minutes. I shall lead you to the top of the cliff, like Gloucester in *King Lear*."

She drew me by the hand in blind silence.

"Now open your eyes."

The panorama before me was astonishingly beautiful. We had reached the edge of the uplands, where the land plunged steeply down into a rich area of lowland country. The suddenness of the change was quite breath-taking. Behind us were the gaunt crags, bare walls, close-cropped pastures and wide moors of a highland area: and before us, hundreds of feet below, stretched out a rich mellow plain dotted with clustering trees and thickly interlaced with hedges. It extended miles and miles into the dim distance. To left and to right the line of steep slopes and rocky cliffs, which formed the boundary of the uplands, was strangely straight.

Again I was taken back mentally to my early days by a resemblance which occurred to me at once, and even grew upon me in fuller detail as I recalled it. I thought of the regular edge of the Hambleton Hills, where they sweep down suddenly into the Vale of York. Indeed, I had tasted this exact experience vividly before, when I was for the first time surprised on the road from Rievaulx to Thirsk by the sudden view from the top of Sutton Bank. The road before us here descended the hill in a series of hair-pin bends. I could almost imagine that it wound forward to Thirsk under the shelter of Whitestone Cliff.

"Annot, we've been here before."

"You will perhaps feel that many times."

"I mean you and I together. Don't you remember that evening drive down Bilsdale, when we turned off through Rievaulx and then got out to look at the view from the top of Sutton Bank? It was here that we stood, just here, and like this. You saw the frightening road ahead of us and urged me to turn back."

"I remember. It was very steep."

"One in four. Quite a motoring adventure in those days. It was sunset when we stood here, and dusk when we drove into Thirsk. We had coffee in a tea-shop in the Market Place. And I say," I added excitedly, "do you remember what you said to me as we stood like this?"

"It's like looking down on another world." She repeated her own words.

"Another world....Look here, Annot, what is it all about? Where are we going? Why have you been sent to me? You haven't told me anything."

"You haven't given me the chance."

It was true. I'd been too anxious to preserve a sham superiority.

"I'm sorry. I'm very bewildered. I don't know what it all means. I hardly expected to begin with a potted tour of my early environment."

"At first many good things from your past life may be given back to you. They will remain to you only so long as you can accept them without evil in your heart."

"Without possessiveness, you said."

"Yes, and without vanity or irritation. You must be on your guard. It is a long journey or a short journey to the City, as you yourself make it. Of course, some good things from your past you will certainly not see again as yet. Those are the things whose goodness you utterly perverted by being selfish and vain about them. Oh, I know you were selfish and vain about everything, in a sense. Certainly I was. But there are degrees of selfishness. And some good things are awfully difficult to pervert."

"You were, for instance."

"It is difficult for any boy wholly to pervert the thing you saw in me—the first revealing of it, the very first. You enjoyed it; you worshipped it; and you didn't merely calculate upon it for satisfactions."

I saw what she meant.

"Perhaps we were parted too soon for that."

"Maybe. I know I wasn't a plaything for your lust. You alone know how far I was a plaything for your vanity."

"There *was* vanity," I said. "Lots of it, of course. I've been reminded of that already."

"You'll be reminded again."

"You're full of dark sayings. Let's go down the hill. You can explain these things as we walk."

I took her hand and we made our way down the steep road together. For a time we walked in silence, as I ruminated on the gist of Annot's remarks. No less interesting to me than what she actually said was the fact that *she* could say it. For I remembered her as a girlish creature, dignified in her young beauty, but delightfully inconsequential in her thinking. This simplicity had charmed me and had seemed to be the expression of her personality. Yet now she was full of wise counsel, and it was not incongruous. Somehow her beauty was fulfilled in this new wisdom. I had to accept it, even though it put her utterly beyond me in the intellectual sphere where I had formerly surpassed her. I knew I had to become her pupil.

"Annot, you know I was never the type for a violent conversion. I never really knew anything about the joys of living consciously in the redeeming Love and that kind of thing. All the same, it's a shock to find myself plunged here into a cold, moralistic atmosphere."

She squeezed my hand.

"Do you call this cold and moralistic?"

"No; but what you say is. In that you're as grave and sober as Confucius. Do I have to struggle towards the City, as you call it, through an arduous course in Ethics?"

"You're a very long way from the City. Otherwise you wouldn't need to ask that. First things first. There may be a good deal of moralising before you come to the second things."

"You think my plight is a poor one."

"I think there's one thing you ought to ponder. You've been taken back straightaway to your youth. That's where I belong in your life, and of course I can only cause you to relive that part of your life which I shared. I'm sure there was some good between us which you need to recapture. Was there also some evil between us of which you ought to repent?"

"Must I relive the evil, even here?"

"You have to reject it. And to that end you may have to relive hours of shame and sorrow; but your repentances will be present to you as well. I have told you that we cannot be other than we were. What was good in our relationship on earth is present to us now. To that extent you are happy. But the evil of it is with you too. Did you try to make me a plaything for your vanity? Did you ever praise yourself in me? Did you sometimes admire yourself even in courtesy and grace to me? In so far as you did, your delight is touched with sadness."

Then I stand self-convicted. That was what I thought: but I did not say it. I had not the courage, I suppose. Perhaps I did not fully understand, as now I understand. My own disquiet was the reliving of such evil as I had brought to our relationship. This thing had come back to me, with the good I had received from it and the evil I had given to it. Of course I had given evil. I had patronised Annot, used her in the service of adolescent vanity, turned her very beauty to a mirror for self-admiration. And there was no penitence from the past to rush upon me and permeate this evil with good. How I longed to be able to recall a penitence, a single prayer—O God, forgive me for my selfishness in admiring myself through Annot.

Her hand tugged at my arm and we stopped. We had reached the bottom of the hill and had entered a little village, a cluster of houses grouped idyllically around a pond. The trees between the buildings filled in what was almost a complete circle. Our own road crossed the edge of the pond by a stone bridge. We strolled on to it and turned together to take in the quiet of the scene.

"This is Blackmere," said Annot, "your first halting-place."

I raised my eyes from the still black pool to the magnificent range of hills we had left behind. They were a riot of colour in the sunlight, the white crags bursting from among patches of green and brown and purple.

"Bracken and heather in the sunshine," I said. "I admit they have always formed part of my dream of Heaven."

"And a pool at our feet," said Annot, as if anxious to keep my attention on what was nearer at hand.

I turned to her. On the gaunt track over the hills she had seemed to be all uprightness and slender dignity. Here, before the pond, I warmed to the rich sweep of her black hair and the shadowed curve from her chin to her neck. She stared silently at the unruffled surface of the pond. I followed her gaze and was rewarded with a sudden inward jab of pain.

"You remember?" she asked quietly.

"Yes, I do now. I didn't at first. It's Threshstone."

At Threshstone, Annot and I had had a memorable quarrel. Standing beside her on the bridge there, with the pond below us, I had stoked up a mood of stupid resentful pique which had culminated in a three-mile walk together of bitter and stony silence. The trouble began when she had refused a kiss; refused it quite rightly with the instinctive revulsion a young girl often feels against the gesture of mastery or condescension which is offered in idle possessiveness. My vanity was injured: and I built up a completely false theatrical situation in which earnest love was damaged and vulgarised by the capriciousness of a moody girl. There was this absurd picture in my mind of genuine love struggling against the instability of a girl's trivial coquetry. My behaviour had been wholly mean, sordid, and self-centred. And at this moment I relived the bitterness of it all, and knew it for a summary and epitome of all my vanities in relation to Annot.

The most devastating thing about this recollection

was my conviction that mere words of apology could never atone. There was nothing to say which could cancel out the evil. The heat of injured vanity, blown to intensity by my fatuous speeches of self-dramatisation on the bridge—it burned again in my fingers and at my ears. The rigid ice-cold tension of that long walk in calculated isolation seemed again to freeze my neck and shoulders in chill immobility. I hated myself; for logic pressed the dejection deeper in an irresistible sequence of thought. If the reliving of this evil is so bitter, if the repenting of it is so hard, even so impossible, what of the vast number of my yet unrecollected sins—the wild pride of my dishonesty, cowardice, lust and conceit? Must each sin be relived in turn, with proportionate shame and proportionate despair?

I turned to Annot in hopelessness.

"I don't know what you've been through; but I don't think I can face it. It isn't just the sins, though they are miserable enough: it's the underlying sinfulness, the rot in the soul."

"God knows our limitations," she said quietly. "We must deal with one thing at a time."

Even that seemed too much for me. I could no more pray for mercy than I could apologise to Annot. The disproportion between the simple prayer and the huge perversion which was me was ludicrous.

"I can't be adequately penitent," I said.

"Of course you can't. No one can. But you can wish to be inadequately so."

I closed my eyes.

"O God," I muttered aloud. "Make me, not adequately penitent, but effectually so."

"Fill up by Thy Mercy," said Annot, "that difference whose magnitude bewilders us."

"The difference?" I queried.

"Between your penitence and the cost of forgiveness."

"By Thy Mercy," I repeated.

And at once I understood a great truth. The joy of recapturing the good through repentance of evil is not the same as the innocent original delight in the good. Innocent delight in the good is gratitude for God's generosity. Joy in recapturing the good through repentance is gratitude for God's mercy. There is gratitude for Creation; and this is what set the sons of God shouting for joy. There is gratitude for Redemption; and this is the inheritance of fallen man.

"I'm sorry, Annot. I was horrible."

"I'm sorry too," she said. "I was not innocent in the quarrel."

"You were in the right."

"I began by being in the right, but I soon perverted that."

"There was nothing to compare with my dramatised indignation."

"There was my dramatised chastity."

The directness and restraint of Annot's statements, even when speaking of her own former faults, made my own attempts at self-criticism look like the self-indulgence of untempered emotionalism. Already my words and thoughts of a few moments ago began to seem charged with theatricality and thereby tainted with vanity. In my very penitence lay something to be repented of—a touch of self-indulgence in the exaggeration of pompous despair, a touch of romantic vanity in the conscious heightening of emotional extremes.

"Even my penitence is corrupted," I said.

"It's all over." I smiled.

"Not quite."

She spoke with gentle decisiveness.

"Surely..." I began.

Her eyes glistened with playful delight.

"You must not be selfish with your penitence. The evil began over a kiss."

I hung my head.

"I know. It was beastly..."

"What shifts you drive me to," she said, interrupting me. "My dear, you must be fair. You have rejected your demand. Let me reject my refusal."

She offered me her hands again. I took them, and we faced each other. Our eyes met without desire. Then she kissed me lightly on the cheek.

"Thus it was," she said. "And it was good."

"Yes. Thank God."

"Thank God," she repeated. "It is redeemed."

For a moment there was silence. Then I could no longer restrain a smile.

"I shall never keep up this pace. The extremes are almost unbearable. I suppose I must believe they're consistent?"

"You must."

"It's hard. When I tried to flirt with you a little while ago, you put on an act that would have frozen Casanova. Now, when I hold you about as passionately as I hold a hymn-book, you begin to shower kisses on me."

"You tried to flirt in vanity," she said. "Now you hold me in penitence."

"Well, I've changed my mind. I'm quite prepared to explore the depths of penitence, if it all ends up like this."

"The marvel of it is that it does," she said. "But I wonder whether you are prepared."

"You'll excuse me for saying so; but it seems a pity now that I didn't spend a rather wilder youth. A sustained discipline in redeeming a series of flirtations would have suited me down to the ground. But alas, my record as a lady-killer is pitiably modest."

"We can't all have the same gifts," she said. "Perhaps you were not lavishly endowed by nature for that kind of success."

"Don't tell me you succumbed to an unaccomplished novice," I protested.

"Well, don't claim credit for restraints which Nature imposed."

"Now you're preaching again," I said. "And I'm racking my brains, trying to recall another quarrel."

"There wasn't another."

"No. I feared not. And I'm hungry for penitence. I suppose I can only repent each sin once?"

"You'll find it's enough."

Though she answered me playfully, I detected an underlying seriousness. She never lost her poise, even when responding to my banter; and the harmony of her personality, in gravity and humour, made me feel scrappy and disorganised. My attempts to be funny, which issued naturally from my cheerfulness, seemed crude and heavy-handed. They were somehow not in perfect harmony with the joy which produced them.

"It's no good," I said. "I'm not equal to it—either the sorrow or the joy. It's bad enough to discover that I'm clumsy in penitence. But to find also that I don't even know how to receive a kiss decently is worse."

"Indeed, you must have wasted your life."

Annot smiled sympathetically.

"That's what I mean," I said. "Even your jokes are funnier than mine. You've got a better sense of humour."

"Perhaps I've merely got a better subject to make fun of."

"No, the difference is in you," I said, trying to make my point seriously. "You've developed a surer touch."

"You mean my kissing has improved?"

I went on, refusing to be deflected by her banter.

"It's as though you'd been to a celestial finishing school."

"But I have," she said. "That's exactly what happens here. You come here just begun; and you have to be finished. Judging from your talk, I should say you'll take a good deal of finishing. So we'd better be on our way." She pushed her arm through mine again and drew me away from the pond, now swinging gaily at my side as we walked.

"It's goodbye to Blackpool," I said.

"Blackmere, please. There's a world of difference. Two worlds, in fact."

And I discovered that it wasn't goodbye. I had seen only half of the village. Having walked a few yards along the lane, we came to a second focus—this time a circular green dominated by a single house, a neat stone building whose pillared portico gave added dignity to what was a fine, square-windowed place of impressive proportions.

"This is our first calling-place," said Annot, as we paused before the circle of grass.

In the middle of the green stood an ornamented iron lamppost. In spite of its exquisite workmanship and design, it seemed oddly out of place. It wasn't that the thing suggested the existence of a gas-works and a gas supply. In fact, that thought never occurred to me. But, in spite of its beauty, it introduced an air of the city into what was otherwise an idyllic rural retreat. As Annot prolonged our pause, I stared at it with a curious interest.

Something suddenly dawned upon me, and I blushed as with injured pride.

"You see what it is?" asked Annot.

"Yes, I do now."

I couldn't say more. I was taken aback.

"It's the old lamppost," she said. "It stood a few yards from my home, near the back gate. Very much beautified, of course, but quite recognisable. It meant quite a lot to us during those few months. We parted under it so many times. I suppose we hallowed it in some kind of way."

I couldn't bring myself to say anything. I was still blushing. It was one thing to recapture the romanticism of youth attached to the hills and dales of my native county. In them were a true grandeur and sublimity which could never be outgrown. But this was quite a different matter. Here I was invited to recapture youth's romanticism attached to a disgustingly suburban corner of an ordinary industrial city. True that city had been my home; but I had long since ceased to relish the vulgarities of its fabric. And what was more vulgar than a gas-lamp at the corner of a city street? Of course, I had romanticised it; but the very memory was embarrassing. In the years since, this particular sentimentality of my youth had been forgotten, while memories of more dignified romantic dreams had persisted. I could not bear to see the vulgar thing redeemed.

"I can't take it," I said.

"You are ashamed," Annot spoke with the same

tranquillity, "because you said goodnight to me under a lamppost. You wish it had been a tree. But it wasn't. We can't alter that. It was a good lamppost and served a good purpose. It gave light."

"Of a kind."

"You studied me very often by its aid."

It was true. Its light had shed magic on Annot's upturned face. I struggled in hostility with my own shame.

"We were city-born and city-bred," said Annot. "We walked together more often among the mills than among the hills. At the time I don't think you minded very much."

"It's as though I'd been invited to a banquet of the gods, and then ceremoniously presented with a plate of tripe and onions."

"No, it isn't," said Annot, "because you don't like tripe. Let's say eggs and bacon. You wouldn't want that dish to be lost eternally."

"You win," I said. "But I hope this isn't going to be the scene of our parting."

"Not yet awhile. I'm taking you to see Manuel."

And we made our way to the door of the house.

2

The room in which we waited to be called by Manuel brought back memories of a different kind and stirred me to some hard thinking. Although much smaller, it bore a very strong resemblance to the waiting-room at my publishers. A table, rather too big for its environment, left as empty space a gangway only about a yard wide all round the room. The only kind of movement possible would have been to march round the walls. Perhaps this was an intentional restriction, for the walls were lined with bookshelves on which books were displayed, not tightly packed as in a library, but faces forward and well separated as in a bookshop window. A few dining-room chairs, standing under the table, completed the furnishings and the general impression that the room had been originally designed for feeding the body rather than the mind.

Naturally I looked at the books. They all appeared to belong to the category classifiable as "religious." Several of the titles and authors' names were familiar to me. Responding to the influence of ingrained habit, I looked round quickly over the whole collection to see whether I was represented myself, and I soon discovered, in the company of the less ponderous volumes, copies of *The Devil's Hunting Grounds* and *Cold War in Hell*. This discovery brought its compensations, but it disturbed me too, for a piece of writing paper had been pushed under the two books, on which was scribbled, *Expected today.* γ+. Now I was quite happy to be expected; but what was I to make of γ+? To the eyes of an educationalist it had the undeniable air of being a mark—and a very modest mark at that. I felt I could have better swallowed γ-. That could have been dismissed as an obvious misjudgment. But γ+?...And the worst thing of all was that this humiliating note prevented me from drawing Annot's attention to what I had achieved since the days of our youthful relationship. I resolved not to bring the volumes directly to her notice, and I pulled out a chair to sit beside her.

"Is this place familiar to you?" she asked.

At least this gave me the opportunity to speak in casually impressive phrases about my familiarity with the exalted spheres in which publishers move and have their being.

"Yes," I said unexcitedly. "It's very like the waiting-room at my publishers. Makes me feel as though at any moment I shall be called into the sanctum, to be told how the sales are going in Missouri and what was said in the latest review from Madras."

Now this was laying it on a bit thick, I admit. I can only excuse myself by pointing out that it was in part my outraged response to the injury of the γ+.

"Oh, you had some books published?"

"A few," I said casually.

She sighed.

"You certainly went out of your way to create difficulties for yourself here."

Bewildered, I remained silent.

"Don't let it worry you," she went on. "Though I can't help you in this matter, there are those who can."

Annot's meaning was by no means clear to me, but somehow her words restored my temporarily disturbed sense of proportion, and I hastily repented of the silly vanity I had just indulged. I had seen too much of more than one world to begin to bolster myself here by reflecting on the achievements of my pen. It seemed all the more extraordinary that these achievements should have been recalled to me at this point. Since they cannot be a call to joy, I said to myself, they must be a call to penitence. I must seek for the evil in them that cries out to be rejected.

But further meditation was denied me. A young lady, wearing a black dress and a secretarial air, came through the door to call me to the presence. I turned to Annot as I rose from my chair, but she remained seated.

"You must go alone. I shall wait for you here."

The young lady conducted me up an impressively wide staircase, cream-painted and red-carpeted. We turned twice in our ascent, for the shallow steps climbed up three sides of the spacious entrance hall in order to reach the balcony of the first floor. To judge from the appearance of the house from the outside, the hall and staircase occupied a disproportionate amount of space. Indeed it became clear, when I was received in Manuel's tiny room, that the building as a whole was really a roofed hall and staircase, with a few little rooms attached as if by accident.

Manuel was very tall, even for an angel. His bearing had that easy dominance and freedom from fuss which the assurance of uncommon height often bestows even upon human beings. He seemed to radiate the tranquil warmth of the large-limbed and large-hearted. There was an unexpected playfulness in his eyes, and the tone of our interview was homely and sympathetic from the start.

I sat facing him, between us his table, cluttered with books and papers. I felt immediately confident that nothing shaming or unnerving was in store for me here, and I relaxed accordingly. It was all the greater surprise, therefore, that Manuel opened on the topic he did.

"It is thanks to your books that you are here."

My relaxation stiffened into tension. There was some catch here. I eyed him in suspicious silence. Was this geniality of manner a device to trap me into vanity?

He rummaged amongst his books and papers and produced a buff card that looked like a Sales Chart. My suspicion became bewilderment. I could see the back of the card as he held it. It was divided into squares and the firm line of a rising graph cut through them.

"You are perhaps surprised to be here," he said. "Yet it is by no means the first case of its kind. A very interesting one, nevertheless."

"I don't understand," I said.

He looked me in the eyes.

"Your books led people to pray for you."

"Oh," I said, nonplussed, yet oddly relieved at the same time.

"Some readers prayed strenuously for your salvation. Others, less confident, prayed earnestly for your conversion. And others again contented themselves with a modest prayer for your repentance."

I smiled, feeling much more comfortable.

"There were also those who prayed God that you might be delivered from vanity, and those who besought Him that you might be given the grace of charity."

I nodded.

"They all helped," said Manuel with a smile. "Even those who prayed merely that your literary style might be purged of its vulgarities."

I hung my head.

"We must hope," he went on, "that their subsequent experience did not lead them to lose faith in the efficacy of prayer."

"I hope not," I said, quite powerfully infected with his good humour.

"Prayers are not always answered in the most obvious way. You know that. For instance, some pious readers prayed that you might be restrained from writing again upon sacred things. You will appreciate that this prayer has now been effectively answered."

"It has indeed," I said ruefully.

"If I may say so," he added, "that is because this view chimed in with official opinion up here."

"Surely," I said, swallowing hard, "the measures adopted to put an end to my writing have been unnecessarily drastic."

He shrugged his shoulders.

"I'm not complaining," I went on, "but a less violent device might have been found."

"Such as?"

I considered the possibilities.

"Well, I could have been deprived of a hand."

"Then you might have dictated the stuff."

"Ah, yes."

"Thus involving another human being in the spiritually hazardous task of writing it all down."

He spoke quite kindly and without the least tone of rebuke. This left me in some doubt how far he was being ironical. Nor was I helped by what followed.

"No. It was necessary to withdraw you from terrestrial circulation. And quickly too. You had dealt with Purgatory and Hell. We saw which way the wind was blowing."

I replied with sad irony.

"My books were more influential than I thought."

"Indeed. They brought about your death. And their readers arranged your destination afterwards." He tapped the buff card. "The figures on your Prayer Chart are quite extraordinary. To think that writing should produce this result in vocal prayer. What a remarkable volume!"

At first I though he was praising one of my books. Then I realised that he was referring to the magnitude of the vocal prayer. He put down the card and leaned over his table towards me.

"You have some questions to ask."

"Naturally I should like to know just where I am, and where I am going."

"We hope you are going to the City. At present you are in the Border Country. It covers a considerable area."

"It is inhabited, I gather."

"It is temporarily inhabited by men and women who, like yourself, have not yet entered the City."

"Shall we all reach the City eventually?"

"We always hope so; but I'm afraid many linger and disappoint us, even at this stage."

I was curious about the mental and spiritual condition of those who lingered in the Border Country, but I could not frame a question about them which would not sound arrogant and inquisitive. So I tried to lead the conversation indirectly round to this topic.

"There must be differences, I suppose, between the outer reaches of the Border Country and the land nearer to the City."

"The end of the pilgrimage is quite different from the beginning. You have just descended from the area known as the *Sacramental Fringe*, or sometimes as the *Platonic Uplands*. Now you are beginning your journey across an area loosely known as the *Ethical Gap*. Beyond that lie the *Sacrificial Marches*, whose far boundary is the coast of the *Joyful Sea*. There is a direct road from here to the coast."

The general picture emerging from this summary seemed to lack a focus so far as I myself was concerned. For, in spite of the significant vocabulary used in mapping the area, the whole programme set before me appeared to be expressible in geographical terms. I could see that a progress was required for entry into the City; but I could not clinch the personal demand in the form of a clear aim.

"For the individual," I said, "I suppose the journeying and sojourning are a kind of test."

"I used the word *pilgrimage*," said Manuel. "There is no examination."

"Then what must I do to enter the City?"

"You must choose to enter it."

"Is that all?"

"In a sense, yes. But I must warn you that choosing Heaven will not necessarily seem as attractive to you when you leave my presence as it perhaps does here and now. It would be wrong not to prepare yourself to face difficulties. If this is, for you, a time of considerable spiritual assurance, you must use it to strengthen your own inner resources against possible periods of temptation in the future. That is sound spiritual advice, here as elsewhere."

"I am in difficulties already," I said, "for I don't know what it means to choose Heaven."

"Of course you don't. In the spiritual life you understand what you choose only when you have already chosen it. That is the mystery of Faith. The more you choose, the more you understand and the more you love. For you can fully love a thing only when you have chosen it. I will put this in a different way, as you know, great truths can always be expressed in a score of different ways: it is only trivialities that can be expressed in one way alone. You will know what you truly wanted only when you have chosen it. This is a necessary consequence of the fact that you cannot understand a thing until you have chosen it. The logic is indisputable. Since you cannot understand a thing until you have chosen it, you cannot know, until then, that it is the very thing you have always truly wanted in your heart of hearts."

"But, even so, I can know beforehand what I ought to choose?"

"Exactly. Will has the primacy over desire. There is a great deal of human unhappiness on earth as a result of the failure to understand this simple truth. For when men allow desire to lead them in pursuit of things which a right will would not seek, they discover that attainment does not bring satisfaction. When they have got what they desired, they realise it is not what they truly wanted. This elementary truth about human nature has too rarely been understood by your thinkers. There is too much talk about man's unsatisfied desires—an absurd tautology, if you analyse the phrase. For desire must be unsatisfied. If it were satisfied, it would cease to be desire. And the notion that a man is the victim of all his idle desires is damaging to human dignity. Man is free; free to make his will lord of his desire."

"I don't understand," I said. "Suppose a poor man wills himself a fortune...."

"That is not willing. That is desiring. Willing is choosing, and choosing is action, while desiring is dreaming. There is no choice unless there is freedom to possess. You may desire a piece of cake in the middle of a desert, but you cannot choose one unless it is offered to you for the taking. And once you have chosen it, it is yours."

"Then if I have already chosen Heaven, it is mine."

"That is exactly what I am trying to explain to you. Insofar as you have already chosen Heaven, to that extent you already enjoy Heaven. That is why, here in the Border Country, you are in part happy and at peace, in part dejected and overcome with shame."

"I have not yet fully chosen Heaven."

"That is the business you are about henceforward."

Manuel watched me carefully as I strove mentally to lay my hand on a simple summary which I might treasure as the fruit of this interview.

"There is only this one condition to be fulfilled. I must choose Heaven, and choose it fully."

"In a sense it is the only condition," Manuel agreed. "But it embraces much that is easily overlooked. For instance, you can enter the City only as a member of a Worshipping Body. You cannot choose Heaven in individual isolation; for that would not be Heaven at all."

I had not thought of this; but it seemed obvious now.

"I can see there is a lot to learn," I said. "How do I begin?"

"You begin by setting out for the City. There is no other way."

I nodded.

"By proceeding on your pilgrimage," he went on, "you will learn what you have already chosen. And, if you do not deaden your heart, you will also learn what you have rejected."

I suddenly felt miserable. The prospect of discovering, item by item, the good things I had turned my back on during a lifetime's selfishness, promised to be purgatorial indeed.

Manuel rose to his feet, and I rose too. Catching the look of misery on my face, he moved round his desk towards me, laid his hands on my shoulders and looked me in the eyes.

"Even rejections can be rejected."

"But they have to be relived," I said hopelessly.

"Wait a moment. When you understand the good things you have rejected, what will you feel?"

"Sorrow, I hope."

"Penitence. And in the experience of penitence you will already have chosen what you formerly rejected. That is what penitence means."

The very pressure of his hands seemed to infect me with gladness and resolution.

"There is joy," he said, "in the presence of the angels of God."

3

When I left the village of Blackmere, again at Annot's side, I was in a more sober mood. Yet, although I had acquired from Manuel a new seriousness of purpose, there was on my part an extraordinary vagueness about the external programme we were embarked upon. I think this was partly due to the complete novelty of my surroundings and the fact that outward experiences here were bound to be of a kind which the newcomer could not possibly anticipate. And I think it was also due to the emphasis which both Manuel and Annot had laid upon the personal pilgrimage in all its inwardness. This emphasis, which had marked their answers to most of my questions, induced an attitude of uncuriousness in regard to externals. The earthly mind would be tempted to label as "subjective" the resulting concentration upon moral and spiritual issues; yet the clarification of all that we were about, in terms of personal reliving and remaking, seemed at the time the very essence of objectivity. And such I know it to be.

We followed the winding road for a mile or two over fairly level ground. Here and there was a roadside cottage, trim and flourishing in appearance. Occasionally, too, I saw gateways which looked like the entrances to more impressive dwellings, but the drives behind them swept round out of sight among trees and hedges. It seems strange to me now that I did not question Annot in detail about these signs of habitation. In view of what followed, it would no doubt have been better for me had I done so. Annot was in a position to teach me a good deal about my surroundings; but the desire not to be her pupil, though no longer prominent in my mind, was by no means totally destroyed. It was not that I was too proud to ask for instruction; but I was still not humble enough to *think* of asking for instruction. And here I must draw attention to a significant thing. Like many others I met on this journey, Annot did not make a practice of giving advice gratuitously. She waited to be asked.

We had reached a stretch of road with open grassland on either side when Annot suggested that we should pause for a while. So we sat down on the grass. It was quiet and peaceful. Nothing seemed to stir. I have known a silence as deep and awesome in a wild remote Scottish glen. Yet here it was felt in the mellow homeliness of a lowland lane.

I looked along the silent road to left and to right.

"I don't think we've met a single living person so far—except in Manuel's house."

"No," said Annot, "but we're going to meet a crowd very soon."

I turned to her with an enquiring look.

"Can you hear nothing at all?" she asked.

I strained my ears in the tranquil stillness. For a brief moment I thought I heard the faint sound of singing. It faded; and then again flowed gently and remotely upon us. There was a mysterious quality about it. I suppose this was due to the complete absence of any human company save our two selves. It brought back memories of childhood tales and legends—about the strains of fleeting preternatural music which lure solitary travellers into the grip of unearthly enchantments.

"I can hear voices singing," I said. "Where are they?"

"It is a group of pilgrims, and they are coming this way. As we left the village I saw them for a moment, winding their way down the road from the Uplands."

"Where are they going?"

"To the City."

Annot spoke quietly, but there was a kind of challenge in her tone. I could not evade it.

"Can I join them?"

"You *could*."

"With you?"

"No; alone."

Again the challenge. I tried to sidestep it.

"*We* are going to the City too, aren't we?"

"They are going there directly. They are a Worshipping Body formed for that very purpose."

Of course the phrase brought back Manuel's warning: "You cannot enter the City except as a member of a Worshipping Body." Here, apparently, was a sudden unexpected opportunity. But it would mean leaving Annot and committing myself to the company of strangers. It would also mean walking straight through this Border Country without any further exploration of its quality and its life.

"I am free to join them or not to join them?" I queried.

"You are free to choose."

In spite of the directness of Annot's utterances, in spite of the unmistakable challenge they contained, I must make clear that they were free from any hint of criticism or judgment. Somehow I was acutely conscious of two facts which on earth would probably have been irreconcilable. I knew that Annot thought I ought to join the pilgrims. And I knew at the same time that she would be quite unchanged in warmth and friendliness if I did not. Without this latter certainty, of course, the decision would have been far easier to make. At the best of times, and in the most trivial circumstances, I have always found it difficult to make decisions. So I resolved to wait and see what the pilgrims looked like. I can see now, looking back, that this was a decision in itself, calculated to lead to one conclusion alone. But at the time I deceived myself that I was merely postponing the moment of choice until the full data were available.

I had not long to wait. The singing grew louder and louder, and soon the pilgrims came into view. They made a fine spectacle. The moving body combined all the dignity of religious ceremonial with the simplicity of a single purposiveness. A crucifer at the front carried a processional crucifix. There were acolytes bearing candles and a thurifer swinging the censer. All these were dressed in albs. There followed a group of men in richly ornamented copes; and behind these came a mixed crowd of men and women, the men all wearing grey monkish cassocks with girdles, and the women in simple white dresses which reached down to their ankles.

"I'm not dressed for this company," I said quietly to Annot, feeling some relief.

"That could easily be arranged," she said, decisively, but without any hint of psychological compulsion.

I do not know that the men in copes were priests, but they acted as cantors, for the whole body was singing the ninety-first psalm antiphonally in Latin. Now I had never been accustomed to worship in Latin, and I was just thinking that this was reason enough to let them go on without approaching them, when a surprising thing happened. The procession came to a halt with the singing of the *Gloria*, and they began to sing a familiar hymn—in English. It was Abelard's hymn, *O quanta qualia*, and the tune was *Regnator Orbis*, so firmly associated with it in my memories. But the English version which they rendered was vastly superior to the one I had known on earth, in spite of the fact that it had to accommodate itself to the most un-English rhythm of the tune.

O how exalted those Sabbaths diurnal,
Kept in the Courts of the Sovereign eternal;
Strong men shall triumph, the weary be rested,
God shall be all, and in all things attested.

There our true City, Jerusalem, is founded,
Peace everlasting and blessing unbounded,
Where hope is crowned in a consummation,
Filling the measure of man's aspiration.

If words can utter the full heart's story,
Let them declare, who partake in this glory,
How great the Sovereign, His high habitation,
How deep the peace and the soul's exultation.

Meantime our minds, lifted up and aspiring,
Yearn for the homeland of all hearts' desiring,
Exiled in Babylon, captive and mourning,
Now to Jerusalem our faces are turning.

There we shall rest from all pain and resentment,

Zion our song and our hearts' contentment:
Thine, Lord, the thanks of Thy people, expressing
Joy in Thy gifts—every grace, every blessing.

Sabbath on Sabbath, for seven days in seven,
Rise up the festal liturgies of Heaven:
Angels and men everlastingly render
Jubilant hymns of unspeakable splendour.

From Thee and through Thee and in Thy decreeing
All things, O Lord, have their substance and being:
Praise to the Father, the Son and the Spirit,
Praise, through the ages the blessèd inherit!

The effect of this hymn upon me was more moving than I can say. It seemed to draw together in a single pattern threads from my life which reached back into many different corners of human experience. The music itself, familiar since childhood, brought back memories of my early days, while the ceremonial procession was a kind of fruition to every religious procession I had seen. I use the word *fruition* purposely in a vain attempt to capture a dominating element in that particular experience. For this procession added something to the sacred dignity which all such rituals possess. There was a sincerity of purposiveness which religious processions inevitably lack on earth. I do not mean that on earth religious processions are either insincere or pointless; but they do lack something that was present here. For the people involved are not really going anywhere. And here, led by candle, cross and censer, the processional body was moving at every step nearer to the Eternal City.

And yet I cannot exhaust the significance which this procession had for me by calling it the fulfilment of a thousand ecclesiastical memories. There was more in it even than that. For the words were Abelard's. As his, they seemed to sum up all that patient seeking and searching which is philosophy, and all that audacious hurling of the brains against the stars which is theology. As his, they bent and tore and battered the tortuous strivings of head and heart into an ordered fabric of disciplined yearning. As his, they were tense and taunt with the conflicting pressures of grovelling rejection and exultant affirmation. For one cannot think of Abelard without feeling the call of the hermitage— the call to solitariness and inwardness, the rejection of the flesh and the annihilation of the self in a stark daily round of prayer and contemplation. Nor is this self-giving the slowly-ripened fruit of an exclusive, lifelong, accepted vocation to the things of the spirit. It is born of the crushed heart and the trampled brain. For one cannot think of Abelard without seeing the face of Héloise.

I stared at the orderly ranks of worshippers, stretching out before me to right and to left. Not one in the whole body had looked at me, or was looking at me now. If there was to be any personal communication between us, then I should have to make the first plunge. The initiative lay wholly with me. There was, therefore, no invitation to human companionship, at least at this stage. There was no evangelical appeal, no open pressure upon me by word or sign. Yet the whole living line of redeemed and committed humanity tugged at my very soul. I knew that, if I were to stand up and say—May I come with you—I should be received with joy and affection. But it would be the end of my cosy sauntering with Annot through the quiet lanes of the Border Country. There would then be no time for talk and speculation, nor for philosophical rumination on the delights and pains of living outside

the Walls; no time for the discovery of how fellow
creatures were erring in lingering before the Gates,
nor for savouring stage by stage the steady progress of
my own spiritual development. It would be all marching and worshipping. Prayer and praise, prayer and
praise, and the relentless pushing forward behind the
unwavering Cross.

Besides, my companions might turn out to be un-
congenial. A lot of narrow-minded spikes perhaps,
who prided themselves on their liturgiology and
whose conversation was limited, at the clerical level,
to where and when and how they had last "said" or
would next "say" Mass; at the lay level, to where and
when and how they had last "heard" or would next
"hear" Mass. How could I commit myself irrevocably
to a company unknown? At any moment a phrase in a
prayer or a common ritual observance might reveal
me to be in a minority of one. I did not know what
they thought of the doctrine of the Immaculate Conception. Indeed, the more I surveyed their faces, the
more I suspected that this company was unlikely to be
congenial in the intellectual sphere. They looked too
cheerful to have read Kierkegaard, too triumphant to
know their Barth. There was a suspicious buoyancy in
their eyes. Probably they had all been brought up on
The Pilgrim's Progress and *The Screwtape Letters*.

A moment before, I had felt that their course was
too hard for me. Now, surveying their glad faces, I
changed my mind. It was all too easy. To put on a grey
cassock and walk straight through the front gate of
Heaven, lost in a massed choir of unreflective worshippers—it was too easy. There are some whom God
saves by suffering. Abelard himself had said that; and
I felt sure I was one of those. I had to struggle to salva-

tion through despair and self-recrimination. I had to travail in the anguish of a Kierkegaard, hacking my route through the laborious stages of life's way. Manuel's own account of the Border Country had given me my cue. I must struggle through domination by the aesthetic until I reached the illumination of the ethical; and then struggle through domination by the ethical until I reached the freedom of the truly religious. I must make my way to light through error. Every standpoint for half-true evaluations must be— not by-passed—but toiled through. There could be no short cut.

Go your ways, I said silently to the Body. Go forward under the Hand of God, and lift up your hearts. Yours is the blessing of simple faith and unreflective worship. Thank God for it. But mine is another vocation. I have trodden the ways of darkness and walked hand in hand with scepticism. There is torment to be endured, desolation to be relived and the cup of penitence to be drunk to the dregs.

The procession had already begun to move again, but in silence now. And an awkward quiet seemed to hang over Annot and myself as we watched the tail of the company gradually disappearing from sight. It was not until they were all hidden round a bend in the road that their voices could be heard once more raised in worship.

"They have gone."

Annot seemed to speak without emotion, yet somehow I felt vastly uncomfortable. In reply, I spoke for the sake of speaking, clutching at one of those oddly unimportant items that reach the consciousness in moods of embarrassment.

"And I don't even know whether they were Roman or Anglican."

"They are all members of the Church Catholic."
Annot spoke simply, and I clutched again.

"I don't think I should have been happy with them."

"Had you been unhappy in their company," said
Annot, "you would have been strangely out of place."

No accusation had been made against me, yet I was
still struggling to find excuses.

"There was something a bit theatrical about it all,"
I said. "Rather like a scene from *Tannhäuser*. I half expected them to strike up the Pilgrims' Chorus."

"If there *was* any theatricality," said Annot, "I hope
you weren't infected by it."

"I don't mean to suggest that they are insincere."

"I'm sure you don't."

"But for *me* to have joined them; perhaps that
would have been insincerity."

"I don't think so." Annot smiled. It was almost
motherly. "Had you joined them, it would have been
because you had chosen to join them. There could be
no insincerity in that."

"But being what I am—and the pilgrims being
what they are—I couldn't have joined them. I mean,
there was too much of a gulf between us. I don't want
to appear to criticise, but the whole set-up was simply
not in my line."

"They were just an orderly body of worshippers."

"Yes, but it was all so impersonal, and rather strenuously artificial. You know I haven't any Protestant
prejudices against ritual. I am always moved by sensitive ceremonial: I'm sure it helps me: but I don't care
to play a part in it myself."

"You prefer it as a background to private devotion."

"Yes," I said eagerly, feeling that the nail had been
hit on the head, and inwardly suspecting that I was
displaying some superiority of piety in an ingenuously

humble way. It was because of this that Annot's next words, sympathetic as they were, struck me like a slap in the face.

"We all have our weaknesses. God understands."

This quiet and utterly affectionate rebuke ought to have stung me to self-knowledge and blown to blazes the little one-man drama I was constructing for myself. But it only served to set my ego wriggling from one fond attempt at justification to another.

"Appearances can be deceptive," I said. "I realise that. But one has to judge by the evidence available. And I don't think they were my type intellectually. It would have been difficult to fit in."

"I'm sure they would have been kind to you."

Painfully ignoring the calm utterances which lovingly put me in the wrong, I stumbled wildly on.

"We shouldn't have had much in common."

"Only the redeeming Love and that Spirit which is the bond of all fellowship."

At last I was silenced. I had been dissected, taken to bits, reduced to débris. Yet the conviction persisted that I was being misunderstood. It was not that my meaning was being distorted. Nor was it that false standards of judgment were being applied. But full allowances were not being made for the peculiarities of my unique personality with its unrepeatable history. Judgments were being passed which, in ninety-nine cases out of a hundred, would have been pertinent and just; but they failed to be relevant to my complex moral and spiritual make-up. Was it possible to put my case clearly and impartially before Annot? I no longer thought so. I studied her calm profile as she sat there beside me, but I could gather nothing from her placid, uncritical gaze and, sensing a new failure of understanding between us, I was filled with a deep regret. I began to be sorry that the procession had even come our way, so close had we been in sympathy before this disquieting episode. The whole thing had been a most unwelcome threat to our companionship, and it had not emerged unscathed from the encounter. Suddenly love for her welled up in me, demanding inexorably some minimum admission from me that I was not what I ought to be. God knows my feeble response was utterly disproportionate to the tumult of self-searching which the occasion demanded; and now I know it too: but I was floundering still in a confusion of shallow and deceptive self-justification.

"Annot," I said, "there isn't only goodness here."

"No," she said, "because there are men and women who have not yet entered the Gates."

"And we bring suffering."

"Yes. We are free to bring a little bit of Hell into the Border Country. But we cannot take it into the City."

"The events of the last half-hour need to be reflected upon." I spoke musingly. "They have certainly not brought pure joy."

"You will have plenty of time to think about them."

I took her arms warmly and looked into her face.

"I may have chosen wrongly, Annot, but I still have you with me. I didn't want to leave you."

For the first time I saw a momentary look of strange sorrow in her eyes. Her eyelids flickered over them, but even as her eyes were closed the black lashes were not still.

"Yes," she said, and her lip quivered. "I am one of the things you have chosen instead."

4

The meeting with Terence was a delightful surprise. We came upon him suddenly, face to face, after rounding a bend in the road. He was walking slowly (I don't think I ever saw Terence move quickly) in that characteristically ruminative fashion. Slight yet compact in build, there was always an air of tension about him which his gentle, languid movements could never dispel. He had one of those faces which improve with age. Small and round, it was too feminine in youth, but when the forehead became lined and the flesh sank so as to bring the cheekbones into prominence, he acquired a certain wistful aesthetic dignity. As a professional musician, he had needed this dignity. As a self-conscious philosopher, he was acutely sensitive to it. And when I say that he was a philosopher, I don't mean that he studied Philosophy, but that he liked to philosophise.

To be honest, I was surprised to find him so near to Heaven. He had been brought up in a Church family, his mother was a deeply religious woman and his sister had entered a convent, but Terence himself had rebelled against the family tradition. Imbued with left-wing idealism and genuinely distressed at clerical stupidity and ecclesiastical corruption, he had early isolated himself in a sad disillusionment too religious in tone to be called scepticism. He had hurt and shocked his mother, whose early hope was that he would be ordained, but he persisted as a vitriolic critic of the whole machinery of ecclesiastical institutionalism and of the essential fabric of Christian dogma. His own temperament and his mother's distress had taken all the buoyancy out of his rebelliousness and left him a sad, even bitter opponent of established religion. There was a long history of earthly argument between Terence and myself on these matters and this gave a delightful piquancy to our present meeting. We greeted each other warmly and there was a touch of banter in our talk from the start.

"You're dangerously near to Heaven, Terence."

"Near is a long way off," he said. "You ought to know that better than I."

"Was it a death-bed repentance that brought you here?"

"Nothing so dramatic as that. From what I hear, it was a lifetime of patient, plodding prayer by my mother and sister." He smiled in a mood of wistful resignation. "I might have guessed they'd be up to that kind of game behind my back. Well, it's their doing. I didn't ask to come here and I'm not going to be made responsible. This business of salvation by proxy is unjust. It makes nonsense of a fellow's freedom. But that's how it is. I never did see eye to eye with God, and I don't expect to begin doing so now."

"No apology can alter the facts," I said. "You're under the very walls of Heaven, almost within earshot of the organised Church at its eternal round of formal prayer and praise. I must congratulate you."

Terence raised his left eyebrow, as he had done a thousand times before in midnight repartee over the coffee cups. He gave a sly glance at Annot.

"You seem to have done pretty well for yourself too."

I thought this might annoy Annot, but it did not ruffle for a moment her inscrutable poise. She smiled at Terence.

"He is no more responsible for his achievement than you are."

"Ah, but I must be fair," said Terence to me. "I must admit now that you were right and I was wrong. I mean, conversion and self-surrender and life in membership of the Church, and all that kind of thing, it really does bring eternal peace. I've seen it. Mind you, though I'm ready to admit the facts, that doesn't mean I approve of them. Far from it. The whole scheme is unsatisfactory. It puts a premium on closing the eyes and fitting in; tying oneself to the ecclesiastical machine without trying to cleanse the thing."

"But does it?" I asked. "I once had a vision of Purgatory, and a pretty grim corner of Purgatory it was too—almost as near to the border of Hell as this is to the walls of Heaven. Now the odd thing is that the place was chock full of clergymen and headmasters and people who had fitted in and got on pretty well in life. You couldn't get away from parsons and preaching, meetings and speeches. Yet here I find the opposite. The way to Heaven seems to be by fields and trees and quiet villages. I haven't attended a single meeting or heard of a single organisation. No one has tried to make me join anything. And whom do I meet? The girl I once made love to, and the man who was always

rude about bishops. No, if there are going to be any re-
tractions, I shall have to grant that I was wrong and
you were right."

Terence was about to protest, but Annot intervened.

"It's very pleasant to hear you both arguing for the
claim of being wrong, instead of for the claim of being
right; but you'll find the novelty soon wears off, and
there are more important things to do. Shall we all
continue together?"

Terence shook his head.

"Not in that direction. I'm happy where I am."

"Are you?" asked Annot.

"You wouldn't be happy if you were happy," I said.
"Pleasantly miserable, you mean."

"Perhaps so. But look here, even if you insist on
going forward, you might take a look at this place
first. There are some excellent people hereabouts.
Come and spend a few hours with me. It isn't far off
the road. You'd be interested to see what's going on
here."

I looked at Annot, but her face was unreadable.

"Is that permitted?" I asked.

"You are free to choose."

"All right," I said. "I don't want to go through the
Border Country blindfolded."

So the three of us turned back. It is a difficult business to try to relate clearly what happened next. The
experience is obscured in confusion and still coloured
in my mind by the shattering bewilderment so soon to
descend upon me. I remember that Terence and I
chatted gaily about old times, and I cannot recall that
Annot said anything. And I remember that we walked
back some way before Terence took us to the right into

one of those openings that looked like the main entrances to big estates. There was a white swing gate which reminded me of a level-crossing. And I distinctly remember turning to Annot as Terence laid his hand on the gate and began to push it open. I had withdrawn a yard to allow Annot to precede me. She smiled at the courtesy and I can even now see her face clearly as she half turned towards me in acknowledgment. A few moments later we were staring back at the closed gate from fifty yards away on the other side. A sudden unnameable sense of loss had caused me to grip Terence's arm, as we walked up the drive, and swing him round to look behind us. Annot was nowhere to be seen. She had disappeared. There was a dreadful certainty in the realisation from the start. The drive wound invitingly into the trees behind us. The road to Heaven lay quiet and untrodden to left and to right. Between it and us the formidable white gate stood like a barrier. And Annot was gone.

I stood for a moment trembling and desolate. Then, feeling the need for some dramatic gesture, I ran headlong back to the gate, determined to scan the road for Annot. But, though I tugged at the gate with all my strength, I could not move it an inch. Sweating with effort and frustration, I started to climb over it, but Terence, who had sauntered after me, laid a hand on my arm to stop me.

"It's locked," I said. "God knows how: but I can't budge it an inch."

"That happens from time to time," Terence said calmly. "It's not intended that we should go through: otherwise it wouldn't be locked."

"It's easy enough to climb."

"I shouldn't if I were you."

There was an awful assurance in Terence's voice that deterred me.

"It wouldn't help matters," he added. "You can see the road is clear."

It was true. I should not get a better view by going over the gate. Annot's presence was a thing of the past.

"I can't understand it," I said. "Can we have offended her? It seems so capricious."

"That's the last thing it is," said Terence, "you can be quite sure. It's intentional and purposive. That's why it's useless to try to do anything about it. One just has to accept these things."

He sighed in resignation, as though the burden of life hereabouts was hard to bear.

"Without a word," I said. "It's almost graceless."

"Exactly. A conjuring trick designed to irritate. It's a prevalent technique among the Citizens. Quite lamentable. If only He could see how much it lowers His dignity!"

"Who?"

"God, of course."

As we began to walk away from the gateway, Terence developed his theme.

"I didn't want to hurt your friend's feelings or I should have spoken plainly before this. The City isn't what it ought to be. I know the people are happy there—but in a very limited kind of way. The conditions of entry are all wrong: they keep out some first-rate people who would be good for the place, men of ideas and originality who just can't bring themselves to grovel. For instance, did you see that procession?"

"Yes, it passed us not long before we met you."

"You weren't tempted to join it?"

"Tempted perhaps, but I resisted. The thing was too

stagey and artificial for me. Besides the people didn't look to be my type."

"Exactly. That kind of thing makes me sick. A whole lot of witless believers can get behind a cross and half a dozen priests and walk into the City in blind acceptance of a mere formula. Give way to the herd instinct and forfeit your individuality, and Bob's your uncle. It isn't good enough."

"I sympathise," I said, "though I wouldn't have put it quite so strongly."

"It can't be put too strongly. The whole machinery of entry is an insult to the human spirit. People who really feel and think for themselves and value their independence are all kept outside."

"Maybe," I said, "but what can one do about it?"

"If one can do nothing else, one can at least reject the indignity of submission. If you fit in, you become a party to the whole set-up. And it's rotten. There's too much trickery, for instance."

"Trickery?"

"You've seen something of it yourself. The way your friend disappeared. It shocked you, and quite rightly. But it didn't surprise me at all. It was of a piece with so much that I've seen. It's unworthy."

Terence spoke with considerable feeling; and what he said had a peculiar effect on me. At one and the same time I felt it was shocking and I wanted him to go on and be even more shocking. There was something in his rebelliousness that chimed in with my own irritation and disappointment at losing Annot. I wanted to have a part in some outrageous protest, yet I had not the courage to hit out myself at the Powers that Be. So I pretended a slight resistance to his words, in the hope that he would reinforce them more violently.

"Surely," I said, "she had the right to leave me."

"She didn't leave you. She was taken from you. It happens time and time again, as you struggle towards the City. It's an endless sequence of senseless, infuriating deprivations. You're given something with one hand and it's taken back with the other just as you are really enjoying it."

"Presumably there's a purpose in it all."

"There's a purpose all right, and it's a damned bad one. To knock all the personality and individuality out of you. To make you curse the day you were born. And I for one am not prepared to do it. Life is miserable enough, and the scheme's a sorry one, but I know that I personally am worthwhile—even if only because I can pass judgment on the indignities and trickeries."

"I can see the indignities," I said, "but where's the trickery?"

"What is it but trickery, when you are continually given things so that you can be tormented by having them taken away? I tell you that's the whole basis of the so-called pilgrim's progress to the City. Time after time you're led up the garden path. You find a girl, or something that seems to offer you the fruition of everything you longed for on earth. Then, just when you begin to possess the joy and fulfilment you have always ached for, the thing is snatched from your grasp. At that moment you're supposed to grovel and say, 'Lord, I am not worthy. This was false idolatry. I was a sinner to pursue it.'—and so on. I refuse to say it, because it's a lie. There's only one reply for the decent man to make—'It was a good thing, God; and it was a damned bad idea to take it from me. If that's Your game, I'm not going to play it.' "

"That sounds all very fine," I said, "but it's not going to bring you peace."

"Peace can be bought too dearly. Dignity and honesty are more important."

"But where is this going to get you? You can't spend eternity criticising God and condemning His whole scheme of creation."

"I don't condemn it. Far from it. I'm on the side of Creation. I think God did a thoroughly good job of work there, and that's why it grieves me to see Him messing it up. Can't you understand? We've got to save God from Himself. That's what I'm getting at. I know Creation itself is good. I say to God—'You gave us love and music and poetry and Nature and brains; and all these are good; too good to be perverted. But when You hit on the plan of dispensing and snatching back these gifts arbitrarily in the interests of so-called soul-training, You abused Your own creation. There was a better way. To grant fulfilment upon fulfilment until You drew Your creatures to Yourself in joy and gratitude and wonder. How much worthier than tormenting Your creatures with capricious deprivations, luring them to Yourself in an agony of aching barrenness.' "

Terence's voice trembled with passion and his meager frame shook, as he clenched his fists and slowly beat the air.

"Oh, God, You might have had free upstanding souls erect in thankfulness before Your Throne. But You chose to have wriggling worms impaled on the points of Your broken promises."

There was a touch of Swinburne about this, I thought. Certainly there was more than a hint of blasphemy; and it frightened me. We were too near to Heaven to start throwing stones. I was afraid because I was implicated in Terence's outburst, having intentionally helped to stoke it up. Now, when I seriously tried to restrain him, it did not prove easy.

"You're being unreasonable, Terence. To accuse God of breaking promises is to charge Him with dishonesty. It doesn't make sense."

"Of course it doesn't; but it's true. Life is a litter of broken promises."

"Whose fault is that?"

"God's. It's His special device for collecting souls. He drenches man with false hopes and dries them up in turn. The hopes of youth, of love, of marriage, of ambition; they're all given to be taken away; they all promise fulfilment, and every promise is broken. There's nothing wrong with man, I tell you. This is God's doing."

"No, no," I protested.

"But all the saints would agree with me. They'll tell you it's God's doing. The Lord giveth and the Lord taketh away. It's His way of luring souls. I quite agree with the saints about that. We don't dispute the facts; we dispute the interpretation. The saints pretend it's a good idea. It isn't. It's undignified and it's dishonest. No decent man would stoop to use the technique. Men win their friends by loyalty and good service—above all, by keeping their word. God wins His friends by letting them down. That's why He gets such rotten friends. Self-respecting people won't stand for it. He ropes in all the riff-raff."

"Come, come," I said. "Think of all the great saints."

"A few golden exceptions. The heroic eccentrics who had a taste for self-immolation. I prefer to think of the common mass of the saved, as I've seen them, in their hundreds, pouring into the City. They're the dregs of creation."

"I won't have that."

"Won't you? But it's God's boast that He specialises in thieves and harlots, publicans and sinners, the failures and the down-and-outs. He doesn't recruit in the West End. He scours the slums and the by-ways. He seeks out furtive creatures skulking in back-streets, and compels them to come in. My good fellow, I know your Faith better than you know it yourself, and you're supposed to be a believer. But I have the sense to see that it's a shoddy Faith."

All this was disconcerting, for two reasons especially. In the first place, I felt that I lacked the vocabulary and the ideas to make an effective reply to it. And in the second place, the whole outburst seemed to have grown logically and inevitably out of a protest which, in its beginnings, I had sympathised with and shared in. The whole tirade was all of a piece—one vast realisation and amplification of the original anger which had made me warm to the first words of protest. I was committed to it. In order to reject it, I should have to reject myself. Of course, I can see now that this view of the situation cried out for penitence. It was useless to resist Terence without trying to annul my own contribution to the outrage. But I did not recognise this at the time. I tried to back-pedal, even pretending that I did not clearly understand what Terence was saying—as though my pious ears were outraged to the point of bewilderment, when in fact the pattern of Terence's tirade was clear as crystal to me.

"I can't think how you can say such things. Meaningless nonsense doesn't become clever by being blasphemous. It's impossible to make head or tail of your charges."

Terence replied with a calm weariness, exaggerating a phrase here and there, like a schoolteacher addressing a dull pupil.

"On your terms, I may be blasphemous. But I'm not incoherent. My complaint against God is cogent and lucid. He gave us a fine world, full of possibilities for human beings to develop themselves, mastering their physical environment, building magnificent civilisations and enriching them with all manner of cultural achievements. He made it possible for quality of hand and brain to assert itself. He encouraged scholars to extend knowledge, artists to create beauty, inventors to devise all kinds of useful implements and machines. He made a world where zeal and toil and idealism could flourish. He established a realm of human achievement. And then He wrecked the whole scheme by decreeing that all self-confident achievement should be unsatisfied; wantonly ordained that no man should taste peace and everlastingness unless he chucked away his own achievement and his own achieving self as so much worthless rubbish, to crawl before his Maker in a dismal pretence of disgusting self-depreciation. He needn't have done this. He's omnipotent. He could have arranged for the good to flower into the better, and thence into the best, without any nonsense of self-abnegation. But He's got a bee in His bonnet about soul-training by means of negations. It's a ghastly mistake, and someone ought to tell Him so frankly."

"How can *you* judge it to be a mistake. What's your criterion of judgment?"

I thought this a clever question, until I heard Terence's reply.

"My good fellow, as I've already said a dozen times, the whole of Creation is my criterion. Everything good that God has made cries out in protest against this single error. If God hadn't made such a damned good show of His positive creation, I shouldn't be able to judge His appalling blunder over this crucial ultimate issue. Credit where credit is due. I'm the first to admit that God gave me the means and the basis for judging Him: but He hasn't a leg to stand on if He tries to deny me the right to exercise what He has given me. I say He's taken the wrong turn; and it's leading Him into a blind alley. He's going to find out, sooner or later, that He's driven all the sound chaps against Him, and His eternal City will be populated by the spineless and the moronic. He wanted a Church Triumphant bursting with brains, guts and initiative—I've no doubt about that. But He'll find Himself with an institution on His hands that looks like a cross between a Borstal and a sanatorium. For His own sake, I hope He has the sense to change His mind."

I must admit that I did not attempt to reply to this. It would have been useless to pretend that I was bewildered, for Terence had made his case as clear as daylight. I was appalled at his blasphemies, yet suspicious at the same time that perhaps more saintly creatures than myself might find them less objectionable. In fact, the thought kept recurring to me that perhaps God might prefer to be fiercely acknowledged and roundly assailed, than to be calmly ignored. Nevertheless I was frightened and uncomfortable. Here was an attempt to slap God in the face and I was guiltily mixed up in it. For, however much my reason told me that Terence was wrong, feelings deeply ingrained in my soul rose in tumultuous and rebellious sympathy with his most devastating utterances. I warmed irresistibly, not just to him, but to what he said. Something which I recognised as the voice of the familiar, established self within me irrepressibly stated its desire—If only God had adopted Terence's point of view!

Perhaps Terence sensed my inner sympathies. At any rate, when he spoke again, it was in an altogether more tranquil vein.

"We must be patient with God, as with an erring child. We must be firm too. Above all, we must not lose our balance. We mustn't allow our irritation to lead us to self-destruction: that's the very thing we're up against. Where God is negative we must be positive. Where God destroys we must re-create."

"You're not alone in your strange idealism, then?"

"No. I've run into a few fellow sufferers who have preserved some shreds of self-respect. They know what to think of the disgusting conditions of entry into the City, and they're only too glad to stay outside. We shall make a stand. Our resources may be limited, but we can certainly show God a thing or two."

"Then you're settling down in the Border Country?"

"You shall see. I've not brought you here for nothing. Look at that."

An impressive, newly-painted roadside signboard was before us, and Terence was visibly proud of its announcement:

> **Border Country Development Corporation**
> **GLENVILLE**
> **The Garden City of the Borderlands**

I was only too ready to quicken my step.

5

Soon afterwards I got my first view of the garden city as a whole. Our road brought us down to the bottom of an open glen, which was conveniently symmetrical from the town-planner's point of view. On the slopes on either side stood red-brick houses, some apparently newly-built, others still under construction. They were all functional semi-detached buildings, neatly sited and lavishly interspersed with wide patches of grass which bordered the roads. It was for all the world like a model Council estate in process of erection. To anyone whose heart kindles at the prospect of well-designed town-planning in progress, the spectacle would have brought delight. Those whose hearts sink before the mechanical sameness and regularity of such estates would no doubt have regretted the insensitive plastering over of the countryside.

The focus of the estate lay in the level area where we stood. Most distinctive of all was a large hall immediately in front of us. This was a red-brick building which looked like an up-to-date wholesale food emporium, but Terence described it otherwise.

"That's our Community Centre. It serves as a home

for social events and such cultural activities as we have managed to inaugurate. At present we have to use it a good deal for public meetings. We're trying to give the whole community the right ethos."

This surprised me a little.

"But I understood that you were a group of like-minded people, already united in your aims."

"We have a nucleus only. Naturally our venture draws people here who don't fully understand what we are getting at. We don't like to refuse anyone. For one thing, we must have builders and labour of all kinds. And in any case we're not going to emulate the City authorities by laying down stupid conditions of residence here. There is a better way. We believe in education."

As he spoke, someone opened the main doors of the hall from the inside, and the sounds of singing reached us.

"They are holding a meeting now," Terence explained.

I recognised the strains and words of *These things shall be*, rendered by what seemed to be a considerable body of men and women.

> New arts shall bloom of loftier mould,
> And mightier music fill the skies,
> And every life shall be a song,
> When all the earth is Paradise.

Trite as are the words and sentiments of this hymn, they seemed to have a stimulating effect upon Terence. This surprised me because I knew him to be a man of considerable literary sensitivity and of impeccable taste in music. It did not occur to me at the time that it was the mere magnitude of the hidden audi-

ence which gave him pleasure. This was to become
plain to me at a painful moment later on.

"You must come and meet Bliss-Witt," he said.
"He's the chairman of our little corporation."

The hall, and its surrounding square, lined with
shops, served in the general design of the estate as the
trunk of a symmetrical tree, from which branch roads
swept up the slopes of the glen among the half-built
houses. I say "half-built" because it became increasingly clear to me, as we made our way up one of these
branch roads, that none of them were actually finished, and only a very small proportion of them were
anywhere near to completion.

Moreover, I could not fail to observe that many of
the unfinished buildings had been unfinished for a
very long time. Although ladders leaned against the
waist-high walls and window frames rose from the
low brickwork, propped up by planks, as if workmen
had left the sites only a few moments before, and although cement mixers stood ready, surrounded by
piles of sand, stacks of timber and heaps of bricks, yet
a closer inspection revealed moss growing on the unfinished walls, and thick rust eating at the window
frames. In some cases the grass was so high around the
cement mixers and heaps of bricks that one knew they
had stood untended for a long time. At one point,
where there was a group of houses roofed but not yet
equipped with windows or doors, I saw birds fly under the eaves as if returning to their nests.

Now I sensed instinctively that it would be bad taste
to draw attention to this mass of unfinished work, so I
kept my thoughts to myself. But it became very difficult to withhold comment entirely when Terence introduced me to Bliss-Witt's house. It had a roof, but

no door and no window panes, and we had to walk along duckboards to get to the front entrance. Here we shifted a tarpaulin curtain in order to proceed inside. And, once there, I was astonished to find that the walls were unplastered and the second story unusable because there was as yet no staircase. Moreover, the first floor lacked floorboards and the ground floor lacked a ceiling. We could see up between the first-floor joists to the rafters of the roof. The furnishing of the ground floor suggested that the occupants had resigned themselves to some degree of permanence in this unhappy state of affairs.

Bliss-Witt, lank, gentle and lazily genial, apparently did not think the state of his home called for any comment from him as host, so, as a guest, I allowed my eyes to rove cautiously at strategic moments and, for the rest, kept my own counsel. Trying to place Bliss-Witt, I imagined he might have spent his life as a literary critic, reviewing biographies and travel-books on the middlebrow fringe for the less arduous weeklies. He caressed his words with his voice and frequently tried to caress them too with his long thin hands. But, after a few tentative gestures, failing to find anything else to get hold of, they invariably sought his own head, and both together caressed that.

"You must make your own Heaven or your own Hell," he said languidly. "We are making our own Heaven, literally building it brick by brick."

My sense of humour came to my rescue here. I could not take Bliss-Witt seriously. It seemed laughable to talk of building Heaven, when they could not even complete a row of semi-detached houses. But I replied politely.

"I see that you have work in progress."

"Our ideal is that no man shall come here and be refused the shelter of a home. To you, as to all pilgrims who come this way, we make our offer—the hand of fellowship, and a roof over your head."

It occurred to me to suggest that there was something to be said for having a ceiling as well as a roof, but I refrained and muttered my thanks.

"We lay down no conditions," said Terence.

"None whatsoever."

"All are welcome."

"Especially bricklayers and plasterers," added Bliss-Witt.

"I see you have need of them," I ventured.

"We have. But we do not complain. We are Heaven's colonisers, Heaven's missionaries, working the virgin soil. There is no goodness without growth. Heaven must grow. No bounds can keep in the glory of it. We look to the day when this settlement of ours will be taken in by the expanding City."

"On our terms," said Terence.

"Oh, of course," said Bliss-Witt. "We must be accepted for what we are; for we have our own unique contribution to make. Heaven will not be complete if we are left outside."

It struck me that, if they were taken inside, Heaven would be even less likely to be complete. But I hesitated to say so, and Bliss-Witt continued in a dreamy voice.

"There must be variety in Heaven. Our Father's House has many mansions."

"In various states of erection!" I suggested.

"Greater Heaven!" Bliss-Witt went on, ignoring my remark. "That is our dream. We are not the enemies of Heaven. We love Heaven. But we hate its walls. We do not believe in walls."

The unintentional irony of this set me laughing at last.

"That explains a lot," I said, and then checked myself, waiting for the outburst. But it didn't come. The two of them continued to voice their aspirations as though I had said nothing.

"The tide will turn," said Terence.

"Indeed, indeed," said Bliss-Witt. "And when our city is finished, God Himself will stand amazed."

"I'm sure He will," I said, and waited for Terence either to laugh, as once he would have done, or to turn on me in anger: but he did neither. He's possessed by this man, I thought, as I saw how their eyes met in a concentration of deadly idealism.

"The conception may outrun the execution," said Terence.

"But a man's reach should exceed his grasp, or what's a Heaven for?" quoted Bliss-Witt.

"It is better to try and fail," said Terence, "than to shrink back shuddering from the quest. We believe in creation and affirmation: we shall not turn to destruction and denial in order to creep within the gates."

"But nothing is finished here," I protested.

"The will is greater than the deed," said Bliss-Witt. "There are houses not made with hands."

"I know there are," I said. "I have seen them. The place is full of them."

"What we have done is well done, in accordance with our great design. We keep our vision pure. We shall never hide ourselves from others within impenetrable walls."

"There's small chance of your doing that," I said, surveying the gaping window frames. "But do drop the heroics and tell me why you can't get on with your building."

Terence's face fell. For the first time he looked thoroughly dispirited.

"The people drift away," said Bliss-Witt, "unequal to the task."

"They prefer the ignominy of abasing themselves at the gates of the City." Terence clenched his fists and there was hatred in his voice. "They are not worthy of our vision. God is too much for them. With all His pettiness, too much for them. He holds the whip."

There was silence between us for a moment. Then, inexplicably, Terence plunged his face between his hands and began to sob aloud. At the same time Bliss-Witt raised his head, as if listening to some distant voice, and slowly nodded it without a word. Something unseen had knocked the life out of them with a lightning blow. I felt myself to be in the presence of some awful revelation, and the tension of my ignorance became unbearable.

"What's the matter?" I shouted. "What is it?"

Terence shrieked back to me in fury.

"Can't you hear? Can't you hear? Christ Incarnate, they're on the move again!"

Bliss-Witt slowly rose and went to the doorway. I followed him in bewilderment: and then I heard. It sounded like the beginning of festivities at a very small village carnival. Two or three cornets were playing a tune, officially in unison. A trombone supplied a bass which, since it frequently registered an open octave or a fifth in relation to the melody, produced a comically hollow effect. The only other instrument was a big drum which thumped out the beat monotonously, avoiding any kind of rhythmic variation. It was crude in the extreme.

"What are they celebrating?" I asked.

"Nothing," said Bliss-Witt. "They're setting out for the City. It's always happening, I'm afraid. Just when work seems to be getting under way, some of the labourers throw in the towel, and off they go. It's the women, you know. They just won't settle here. They find it uncomfortable, things being as they are, and they're too impatient to wait. They get to work on their menfolk. And there are always one or two spies who come this way without any thought of settling outside the City. They stir up the others, and there you are."

A procession came steadily down the hill, in odd contrast with the previous procession I had seen. The only ritualistic touch was provided by a banner, carried at the front. This was a vulgar yellow thing, with a cross and the words WASHED IN THE BLOOD OF THE LAMB worked on it in a hideous scarlet. Behind the banner walked the small band of instrumentalists. They had made for themselves uniform caps with scarlet bands, and each one was attached to his instrument by a scarlet sash. For the rest, everyone was in ordinary workaday clothes. And the "rest" consisted of thirty or forty men and women of unmistakably proletarian taste and habits.

As they approached, they began to sing:

> Flowing over, flowing over,
> My cup is full and flowing over.
> Since the Lord bless'd me,
> I'm as happy as can be.
> My cup is full and flowing over.

One or two of the more fervent members of the body, who appeared to be more accustomed than the rest to this red-hot brand of evangelical piety, accompanied

the words of the hymn by pantomimic gestures of a
stereotyped kind. They waved their hands sideways
(*Flowing over*) and held an imaginary cup in their
hands (*My cup is full*); they pointed upwards to the
Lord (*Since the Lord*) and then down to their own
chests (*bless'd me*). Finally (*I'm as happy as can be*)
they clapped their hands rhythmically together. This
performance reminded me of the ritual we used to
adopt for concerted renderings of *Underneath the
spreading chestnut tree*, but it accorded little with my
notions of memories of public worship.

Bliss-Witt, standing beside me, leaning against the
doorway, shook his head slowly.

"They will sing themselves into slavery. Morally it's
indefensible. And aesthetically it's unspeakable!"

The spectacle did not inspire me. I found it faintly
ridiculous. Yet, at the back of my mind, I knew that I
ought to feel otherwise. These people had made their
choice. They were going towards Heaven. Though
they sang neither the ninety-first psalm nor Abelard's
hymn, their decision was fundamentally the same as
that of the other pilgrims I had seen. Whilst *I* lingered
in Glenville. What was I doing here? Finding out
about the quality of life hereabouts, I hoped, with a
view to eventual entry into the City. But what need
was there to explore the Border Country thus? Manuel
had given me the answer. So that I should know what
I had chosen.

This last thought made me shrink in shame. Was
this, then, what I had chosen; the Garden City of the
Border Country Development Corporation, this litter
of unfinished buildings, this fatuous dream of an ex-
tra-mural model estate? Could it be that there was
some hidden connection between the impulse which

had diverted me from the heavenly highway and this
tawdry symbol of a frustrated endeavour to outwit
God? Was there some inescapable logic linking my
failure to join the first band of pilgrims with the outrageous blasphemy of Terence and Bliss-Witt? They
thought they knew better than God. Was that my case
too? But I had laughed at Bliss-Witt, found him ridiculous. And found this procession ridiculous too, which
was setting out for the Eternal City.

Amid the clash of thought and counterthought, one
thing stood out clearly in my mind. I had already rejected one opportunity to join a pilgrim-body, and the
rejection had brought me to this epitome of rebellious
triviality and frustration which was Glenville. If I rejected a second opportunity, I should come to regret it
even more. I turned to Bliss-Witt and stupidly drew
him into it.

"I've half a mind to join them. Do you think they'd
have me?"

"They'd have you all right. Give you a banner to
carry, if you're so minded. Should your talents lie in
that direction, they may even have a spare cornet."

I laughed. Bliss-Witt might be on the wrong track;
but he was no fool. This little body might be going the
right way; but they were hardly my cup of tea. Had I
failed to join in the singing of *O quanta qualia*, only so
that I could fall in behind a third-rate imitation of the
Salvation Army to the strains of *Flowing Over*? The
plan was absurd. But even as I rejected it on these
grounds, *Flowing Over* fell out of the scheme. The
band of pilgrims was rapidly disappearing in the distance, as they turned into Community Centre Square,
to make their way along the road to the Highway
which I had trodden so lately with Terence. Barely au-

dible, the strains of *Tell me the old, old story* came
floating up the hill. The thing gripped me with a
longing of which I was immediately ashamed. It was
the street lamp at Blackmere all over again. For the
sentimental hymn took me back to my first Sunday
school, in a downtown parish on the dingy fringe of
industrial slums. I had known the hymn by heart before the age of six. And I suddenly saw my mother and
father meeting me at the school gates, to take me for a
Sunday afternoon walk.

I ran across the duckboards to the gate, stared down
the now empty road, and strained my ears to catch the
music from the lost and rejected body of worshippers.
Even as I did so, I knew that it was an idle dramatic
gesture, vainly designed to conceal from myself the
fact that no action had been taken. I had rejected
action, and this was a way of covering my rejection
up. This was a way of trying to snatch some morsel of
the emotional satisfaction which accompanies decision from an experience in which decision had been
evaded. This was a way of trying to get the feeling—I
long to go with them—from the experience of refusing
to go with them.

Bliss-Witt smiled at me from the doorway.

"If you really want to do a sprint after them down
the hill, I think I could lend you a mouth-organ."

He knew my dramatic gesture for all its futility. He
mocked me because he saw that I was indulging in
hollow emotionalism. I deserved the mockery. I am a
worm and no man, I said, the very scorn of men and
the outcast of the people. And, being a worm, it is
natural that I should have to crawl into the City.

This very obvious corollary struck me as a bright illumination. It provided the appropriate metaphorical

answer to Terence. I returned indoors and stood over him, still slumped in the armchair.

"There's a simple reply to you," I said. "It's at our best that we know we're worms. And we must enter the City at our best. Therefore we must enter as worms. Crawling is the only way."

Terence waved his hand in deprecation.

"Two and two make four. That's the kind of 'best' God has chosen for us. It's a bogus 'best.' Only a third-rate God could have thought it up."

"Oh," I said, surprised that my point was so easy to counter.

"Is that all you have to say?" Terence sneered, and I resented it.

"No," I said decisively. "I'm going."

"To the City?"

"I hope so."

Before I plunged finally through the tarpaulin screen, I turned with a last impulse of sympathy.

"Will you join me?"

He rocked in the chair with hysterical laughter: and I left him.

6

The gate was open again when I reached the Highway and soon I was walking once more in the right direction. Naturally I felt a good deal chastened. My deviation had brought me into the presence of a thundering absurdity. Moreover, it had cost me the company of Annot. As I walked along in solitude, I was miserably conscious of all the questions I had failed to ask her. I had neglected to enquire what it might involve to diverge from the Highway. I had not even sought from her any picture of what lay immediately ahead. So that now, as I walked alone, the only purpose I could cherish was the colourless one of knocking the miles off on a quiet road.

It was with relief, therefore, that I came upon a massive billboard, erected on the edge of the Highway itself. I stared at it in amazement and delight, for it seemed to offer the answer to my deepest need.

PILGRIMS TRUST INC.
(Under the patronage of the Friends of the City)
ORGANISED PROCESSIONS
to suit all tastes depart for the City at
regular intervals.
No Wayfarer Refused.

Entrance to Encampment Fifty Yards Ahead.
There is a place for YOU.
Apply at the Enquiry Bureau.

The clerk in the little hut labelled *Enquiry Bureau* was most helpful.

"You have come at a most opportune moment. Several processions are now preparing to set out. Come along."

A few moments later we were walking up a little side road, trim and formal enough to be called a drive.

"There's sure to be something to suit you. We rarely find anyone who won't fit in somewhere. Of course, it's just possible that you may have to wait a while; but you wouldn't mind that. There's plenty to do hereabouts." He pointed to a small notice-board at the side of a wicket gate.

PILGRIM'S PROGRESS
Guided tours along the route taken by
Mr. J. Bunyan.

"Is it all above board?" I asked apprehensively, and then, fearing lest I appeared rude, added, "I mean, does it meet with the approval of the City Authorities?"

"We conduct people to the City. Surely that answers your question."

"It all seems rather commercialised." I spoke tentatively.

"Poor commerce," he laughed. "We're a non-profit-making body started by the Friends of the City. Look at this."

He gave me a leaflet, published by the Trust, and pointed to some items on the second page.

SOME UNSOLICITED TESTIMONIALS
FROM SATISFIED USERS

"...Before the very Gate of Heaven I pause to say Thank you to the Pilgrims Trust. You are doing a great work. I never expected to get here...." (Mrs. J. W., late of Wigan.)

"I spent my life in moral squalor and spiritual sloth. I was never expected to recover...Clergy said my case was hopeless. It is thanks to the Pilgrims Trust that I am here today...." (P.P.S., late of W.C.I.)

"...I roamed the Borderlands in solitude for many years. Nothing seemed to do me any good. Then a kind friend told me about the Pilgrims Trust. A thousand thanks. I can hear the harps already." (Rev. G.G.B.)

There was no opportunity to question the clerk further. We had arrived. It was an enormous field occupied by a number of massive marquees.

"There is a different kind of fellowship in each marquee. You are at liberty to choose between them. They are all numbered. This board will give you some idea what they stand for."

So he left me, standing under a great contraption that looked like a cross between a cricket scoring board and a main-line station traffic indicator. It was incomprehensible, but sufficiently fascinating to stir my curiosity.

TABLE OF DEPARTURES

Body	Marquee No.	Departure
Ritualistic	1	Imminent
Pietistic	4	Preparing
Aristocratic	2	Imminent
Modernist	8	Not fixed
Evangelical	3	Preparing
Fundamentalist	5	Not fixed

My first impulse was to try to memorise this list and

then to do the rounds systematically. But the effort proved too much and the immediate surroundings too interesting. I moved up to the first marquee. Coloured pennants hung from two posts before the entrance, and a banner stretched between them was inscribed with the words *AD SANCTAM CIVITATEM*. Two or three horses tethered nearby were equipped with colourful saddle-cloths. These prepared me in some measure for what I encountered inside the tent.

There were men in albs, men in copes, men in cassocks and laced cottas, and one even wearing a mitre. A row of golden censers hung from a rope, and portable candlesticks leaned against the canvas. Those who were not wearing ecclesiastical costume were dressed in mediaeval apparel of all kinds. Men and women moved before me in every brand of Plantagenet finery, so that the place looked like a dressing-room for a historical pageant. It was as though I had stepped suddenly into the world of the *Canterbury Tales*.

Two friendly-looking persons approached. They might have been father and son. The elder clapped me on the shoulder.

"Give ye good-den, sirrah."

"Oh...how do you do," I said awkwardly.

"We go to seek the Holy City, accoutred like the knights and palmers of old."

"So I understand."

"Then doff thy dreary apparel and join our goodly band."

"I can't see anything wrong with my clothes."

"The barbarous trappings of a wanton and a godless age, fit only for the paynim or the rude-fingered hind. It ill beseemeth knight or vassal to venture forth in quest of the Holy Grail apparelled like a clerkly steward of the Welfare State."

The younger man perceived my embarrassment and
intervened on my behalf.

"Good Uncle Wendle, vex him not with thy raillery,
for i' faith he is grievous cheerless of mien."

"Beshrew me, coz, if I meant him any ill. Nathless I
confess thy rebuke toucheth me nearly." He turned to
me. "Join us, good sir. We go to enter upon an inheritance past all men's desiring, more rich than the
choicest domain of earthly baron, fief and forest,
champaign and tillage."

A young lady joined us at this moment. Her rich
bodice and high head-dress gave her the dignity of a
queen. As she took the arm of the younger man, her
long furred sleeves swept the ground. He gently patted
her hand.

"My fair Leonora, let thy chaste eyes work their
wizardry upon this vagrant wight. We have urged him
to make up the number in our retinue. Plead with
him, lest he turn aside unwittingly from his own soul's
bliss."

The lady gazed up at her lord. I almost expected
them to burst out into a duet from *Il Trovatore*.

"Eustace, good my lord, I can gainsay thee in nothing. Thou didst raise me from the lowly cot, to deck
me in jewels and set me at thy right hand. For me thou
didst forgo the wealth offered in dowry by the lady
Isabella."

This seemed to me to be a digression irrelevant to
what had gone before, but it immediately absorbed
the interest of Eustace.

"By'r lakin, I had been parlously undone had Isabella shared my board and bed. She was as testy as a

vixen as ever drew curtain in lady's bower. Nay, good wench, I will speak home. Thou art my soul's treasure. Thou hast dowered me with thy heart and hand, and what availeth the power of wealth before the searchings of our lady Venus? Thou too didst turn thy heart from nobility and riches. Didst thou not deny the great lord Dubois? How oft did I see him, astride his barbary jennet, pricking o'er the plain towards thy humble dwelling! How I did fear lest he might win thy heart with his boasted exploits. For a valorous knight he was and a garrulous, whose talk was all of venerye and derring-do. Forsooth he slew mighty monsters with his falchion and hung his walls with the bones of his victims. Yet thou wouldst have none of him, for all his pelf and chattels. Thou dravest him wode with thy gainsaying, till he betook himself to a desert cell, and there became a holy hermit."

As a writer, I have always been on the watch for copy, so that the private history of Eustace and Leonora was rapidly becoming a matter of some interest to me. I was therefore not displeased to see the lady shake her head slowly in reminiscent fashion that seemed to promise a further instalment of this gripping serial.

"The heart of Dubois was all awry. There was no surety of good renown for maid or dame within his household. He offered love, but not the name of wife. His hand was bounden to another. I could not have lived to see the daughter of my father wanton it in dishonour with the spouse of another, were he churl or noble. Besides, I will not play upon the second viol to any she that lives."

The two speakers were by this time completely oblivious of the aim which had originated their intimate colloquy. My interest was matched by Uncle Wendle's impatience.

"Gadsooks, forsooth and by my halidom," he said. " 'Od's bodikins, forebear, forbear. Ye prate of naught but dalliance and the ravishments of love. Ye toy and prattle as ye were swain and milkmaid a-wooing neath the vesper star. Beshrew me, and Dan Cupid hath not witched you both for all time and eternity. Away, and disport yourselves privily, where your fond japes disturb not our graver discourse."

The two withdrew obediently a few yards, and I saw Eustace take up a lute. He seemed to sing quietly to Leonora, gently thrumming the instrument. Uncle Wendle brushed his eye with his hand.

"There is neither grief nor sin betwixt them. An it be true that the hearts of the saved are as the hearts of childer, it will not be long ere these twain foot it featly in the pleasaunces of Heaven."

For myself, I felt that if simplicity of heart were a qualification for entry into the City, first places were not likely to be given to people who were permanently engaged in the performance of extempore musical comedy. Uncle, however, continued to speak with emotion.

"Ah, there will be mickle joyance there and all manner of spritely delectation. Wilt thou not come too?"

At last I had the chance to clear up one point at least.

"Excuse me. I'm a little confused. The dress and language adopted here are naturally something of a surprise to me. Did you live on earth during the Mid-

dle Ages, or did you live in my own century—the
twentieth?"

"We are all thy compeers of the twentieth century.
But we shall not bemean the courts and terraces of the
Most High with the talk and trappings of an age given
over to lust and lucre."

"I see that point," I said. "But the young man spoke
to the lady of their past life in very misleading terms.
For instance, he mentioned a noble who rode to visit
her on a barbary jennet. Presumably this was poetic
licence?"

"Aye, thou hast hit the mark. It was no barbary. To
speak plainly, sad brow and true maid, it was a Vaux-
hall Velox."

"Oh, I see."

I was a little taken aback.

"Then this man Dubois," I said, "who sounded like
a mixture of Beowulf and Sir Mordred, was presumably not engaged in such bloody pastimes after all?"

"No, he was a man given over to more peaceable
pursuits."

"What in fact did he do?"

For the first time Uncle Wendle's voice had a completely familiar ring.

"Something in Football Pools," he said.

I felt I was beginning to get the hang of things.

"Certainly very prosaic," I said.

"Prosaic, quotha! Nay, the lips of man are sullied in
speaking thereof."

"Yet," I added, looking round on the brightly costumed assembly, "I find it difficult to realise that all
these people were my contemporaries. That man, for
instance; he's a bishop, I suppose?"

"Never a more lordly prince of the Church fathered his faithful sheep or drove out the heretic with candle, book and bell. A noble prelate and a gentle pastor, he gave of his benison freely to the widowed and the fatherless. He was as gracious a pontiff as ever wore mitre at the altar or bore crozier through the streets."

I wondered which episcopal throne he had graced.

"One of the ancient sees?" I queried.

"Suffragan of Haliwyke."

I couldn't help suspecting that the prelate in question had spent more episcopal hours in filling up forms than in bearing his crozier through the streets. But I didn't say so, for a formal little trio came up to us—a priest, wearing cope and biretta, his hands held together before him, and two attendant servers in cottas, who held open the cope.

"*Pax vobiscum.*"

The priest gave a slight bow and then made the sign of the cross over me.

"Father Thomas," said Uncle Wendle.

"So called," said the priest, "neither after Didymus, nor yet after our blessed martyr of Canterbury, but after the angelic doctor, *patronus meus.*"

He removed his biretta, kissed it and handed it to one of his servers.

"He is versed in all manner of learning," said Uncle Wendle. "The feathered songsters of the dawn speak not more ravishingly to the soul than he. Would he might win thee to be of our company."

"*Nihil obstat,*" said Father Thomas.

"Except that I don't quite fit in here," I said.

"Ah!" Father Thomas waved his right hand imperiously at Wendle, indicating that he should leave us. I thought this rather rude, but Uncle bowed politely and departed obediently, apparently no ways ruffled.

Father Thomas fixed me with his eyes, and his face slowly stretched and creased itself into an enormous smile.

"Our Holy Mother the Church is waiting to receive thee and clasp thee in her arms." He stretched out his hands in a semi-circle, as though the Church and he were synonymous.

"I count myself one of Her sons," I said.

"Then make your peace with Her in the confessional, that She may carry you within the Gates. Our Lady, Saint Thomas and all the saints will intercede for you."

He spoke with the confidence of one who knew their intentions.

"There are too many differences between us."

"*Extra ecclesiam nulla salus.*"

"I'm not disputing that. But I'm not ready to fall in with you."

"The Church, of Her bounty and Her wisdom, will make up all that is lacking in your self-offering."

"Even She will find her resources strained."

"She can call upon an inexhaustible treasury of merits."

"My difficulties are not theological," I said. "They're aesthetic. The whole conception behind this procession is unsound. I've no objections to this ecclesiastical ceremonial. That doesn't upset me. It's the laymen. I can see the point of their dressing up. I'm sure it makes everybody feel elated. But need they try to talk like characters in *Ivanhoe*?"

"We go to the Holy City; and we go with music in our hearts and poetry on our lips. Would you have them talk like characters in *Ulysses*?"

"If it must be one or the other, I suppose there's something to be said for *Ivanhoe*. But they're not the only alternatives."

"These, our sons and daughters, have eschewed the prosaic. Their speech is part of an all-embracing ritual of dress, gesture and voice."

"There's no virtue in exchanging plain prose for bad poetry."

"Are you sure of that, if it happens to represent the movement of a simple soul towards self-transcendence?"

"I'm sure that the result is pure vulgarity."

"Come, come," he said, "this argument of yours could be used against all earthly worship and ceremonial which fail to satisfy strict aesthetic demands. Is it better that the church choir should not sing at all, than that they should sing out of tune? Is a plain-clothes assembly more pleasing to God than the cheap vestments and tawdry colours of a slum sanctuary?"

I began to feel beaten; but I had one card left.

"We are no longer on earth," I said.

"We are not yet in Heaven. These people have striven in worship throughout their lives after an ageless splendour which they could neither localise nor grasp. They strive still, within the limits of their own spiritual and intellectual development. They have moulded a speech which is a symbol of their escape from a drab, unexalted corner of finitude. They rejoice in it, because its fineries and false archaisms seem to raise their personal interests and social relationships nearer to the level of the splendour they glimpsed in their earthly sanctuaries. That splendour was too often vulgar and bogusly archaic." He pointed to his own magnificent cope. "The time will not be

long, I pray, before this too will seem another vulgarity, laughably absurd before the splendour of the Most
High."

"What then?" I asked.

"Then will be the time to burn it to ashes, not in arrogance but in humility, not in rage but in laughter."

"Meantime," I said with a light irony, "the more
rhetoric and tinsel, the better."

"Meantime, we endeavour to express our worship
and exalted fellowship with all the means we know,
groping after the dignity of Citizenship with such
poor makeshifts as these which you criticise. We are
still rooted in our earthly personalities. It may disturb
you that we cannot at once escape the intellectual and
cultural inequalities of our upbringing in time. Perhaps it ought to disturb you more that we cannot at
once shake off the inequalities of our spiritual development on earth."

There was a rebuke here; but I was distracted from
digesting it, for suddenly a trumpet call rang through
the tent. Everyone fell silent and the trio before me
turned their backs upon me, in order to face the far
end of the tent, where a herald put down his silver
trumpet and unrolled a scroll.

"Attention, good men and true. Be it known to all
hereby that this is the order of our going in the solemn
procession. Heralds and pursuivants go before, succeeded by armed and mounted knights. Acolytes and
thurifers follow next, succeeded by clerks in minor orders. Lay brothers and priests follow next, succeeded
by women who have taken vows. Then follow, borne
in all due dignity and reverence, the sacred relics of
Blessed Constance Wolfstone. At a decent distance
there follow the Bishop and his attendants. The laity

bring up the rear, the nobility leading and the commonalty succeeding. Let all prepare to take their places!"

During the confusion of movement which followed this announcement, I slipped quietly and unobserved out of the tent.

7

It is difficult for me, in view of my personal prejudices, to do justice to the people I encountered in the second marquee I visited. For they seemed to represent a point of view with which I have never had the slightest sympathy, attaching importance to things which, in my opinion, are utterly trivial, and treating with unconcern the things that are weightiest in my eyes. But it is important that I should set down honestly what I saw, for as I now realise, the character of the Border Country was being gradually revealed to me: and in appreciating that character, I came to believe that I was learning something about the quality of life within the City itself.

For instance, what I saw in the first marquee, together with my experience of the strange settlement at Glenville, led me to expect a quality hereabouts which I am tempted to call "caricature." Yet it is not really the right word. It suggests ridicule of a destructive kind, and in fact there was something very constructive about the whole experience. Human qualities, notions and habits of mind were somehow accentuated to the maximum they could endure without being distorted into something else. There was no distortion; only a kind of ruthless intensification. It was as though people were being impelled to follow their own tendencies to some definite and logical conclusion which was inexorable. The kind of vivid, intensified behaviour which resulted had, for me, a faintly ridiculous flavour; but I was never happy to dismiss it as merely ridiculous.

Thus I had seen at Glenville a fundamentally pelagian rebelliousness against penitence carried to a frightening and yet illuminating fruition. It was easy to see the moral of that. But what of my experience in the first marquee? There was nothing in what I saw there that I could point to as evil or heretical, yet I found it absurd in many respects. Was there something there to be rejected? My Protestant upbringing had made me a little squeamish at the sight of the ornamented casket resting on a rich cushion, which I saw was to be borne under a canopy at the heart of the procession, and which, I now know, contained the relics of a minor saint. But it would have been irrational and impious to object because these people were to march to the City bearing the richest treasure they had as their offering. Again, their talk was stilted and the clothes, at least of the laity, reminded one of a fancy dress ball. Yet they plainly enjoyed the assumption of new roles as the fruition of some long-unsatisfied longing to escape from a drab and discourteous world. No doubt their mediaevalism was historically inaccurate in relation to speech, manners, and churchanship; but that was no bad thing. A dream was being realised, and taken for all in all, it was a better dream than most that possess the heart of man. In short, though I was quite unable to throw myself into the pageant-life of the first marquee, I felt a sneaking regret that this was so.

No such regret touched me for a moment within the second marquee. I was ready to leave as soon as I entered, but I forced myself to linger and see all, as one forces oneself through a boring book which one ought to read. The only thing remotely connected with what I had seen in the previous marquee was a large shield, suspended inside the entrance. It was inscribed with the words *NOBLESSE OBLIGE*, yet in appearance and design the thing struck me at once as more like the emblem of a twentieth-century school than the emblem of fourteenth-century chivalry. For the rest, I was plainly among my own contemporaries. A very large number of the men wore morning suits, with toppers either in their hands or on their heads. Rather incongruously, many of the women were costumed in autumnal tweeds and wore flat-heeled shoes. It occurred to me that this apparel was eminently practical in view of the long walk before them. They would certainly have an advantage over the men. But there were also groups of men and women in athletic attire. Perhaps the most amusing was a small band of full-grown women who were wearing gym-slips. Their lavish hips and thighs, and their close-cropped hair, gave them a barrel-like appearance. One felt they ought to be rolled towards the City. Another small group of women were more decorously draped in the Grecian tunics popular at classes in eurhythmics. Attractive as these tunics can be, it was unfortunate that in this case they had been adopted by the sparer and more angular ladies. This failure in dress-sense produced something like a posse of scarecrows.

Male costume in the twentieth century less easily

leads to such indignities. A group of men in rowing sweaters, with shorts and bare legs, coloured caps and scarves, looked athletically impressive in spite of the fact that they mostly appeared too old to face the rigours of their sport. Nevertheless each held an oar, which he leaned upon as it rested on the ground, and the freshly-painted blue blades added a welcome touch of ceremoniousness to the scene.

A group of men in cricket attire were engaged in the extraordinary job of distributing bats to the men in frock-coats. As each gentleman received his bat, he held it blade upwards before him as one would hold a processional cross. I was driven to the almost incredible conclusion that each of these frock-coated gentlemen was destined to bear this symbol before him in the forthcoming procession. This belief was reinforced by a remarkable little ceremony which followed upon the distribution of the bats. A suave voice said, "The Straight Bat, gentlemen, please!" and immediately the dark-suited gentlemen took their places in a straight line, two abreast, straightened their toppers on their heads, and solemnly raised the bats before their eyes, the blades facing forwards. One of their number walked along the ranks, gently adjusting a bat here and a topper there. This rehearsal over, he said "Thank you" and the gentlemen relaxed into their former dignified disorder.

Now one advantage—sometimes a doubtful one— of being in the company of people of this ostentatiously cultivated kind, is that in public places they talk so loudly to one another that the bystander can learn their business, their interests and often even make a rough guess at their I.Q. without the trouble or indignity of conscious eavesdropping. They have an

ingrained habit of talking with especial clarity and
emphasis for the benefit of strangers who happen to
be about, without registering any open knowledge of
their presence. Thus two aristocrats near me per-
formed, as it were, an extempore little dialogue, with
myself as their tacitly recognized but unacknowledged
audience.

"I look upon it as the last great race, Willoughby."
The speaker, a man of immense proportions, swayed
back on his heels to what seemed a perilous angle from
the perpendicular.

"That's the man's view, Conway: and it's absolutely
right." Willoughby nodded in reply with a gravity of
expression and movement appropriate to the utterance
of profundities.

"We're all in it together," said Conway, "shoulder to
shoulder." And he uplifted his splendid chest as if to
reassure his slighter companion about the quality of
their joint resources.

Willoughby's heavy face continued to rock in ponderous agreement.

"Come rain or sunshine, we're ready," he said.

"All set for the starting-pistol," Conway added,
warming to the metaphor. "I never felt fitter. And, after all, a man's only as old as he feels."

"He is. You've put it very neatly, Conway. As old as
he feels." And the acquiescent facial rocking was ac-
celerated.

"We love the game above the prize."

"That's the sportman's view, Conway; and it's absolutely bang on."

"Win or lose, Willoughby, we've got to stick it to the
last ball."

"To the end, Conway. You've put it in a nutshell."

"I'm not a fellow for sentiment," said Conway, delicately exploring his grey silk tie with the thumb and forefinger of his left hand, "but there's such a thing as playing the game."

"There is, there is. It's what makes a man."

"A straight eye and a steady hand, and first thoughts for the team, Willoughby."

"The team always first, Conway."

"I'm not a fellow for religion, Willoughby; but God give us the the guts to see this thing through!"

"With clean hands," said Willoughby.

"With clean hands," Conway repeated emphatically, and then he suddenly infused a velvet gentleness into his voice, "if only for the sake of the ladies."

"The ladies!" Willoughby repeated the words quietly, wrapping them in a breathy reverence which issued from the throat. "That's the gentleman's view, Conway; and it's dead right."

"They have their own way of looking at this, Willoughby—crowns and angels and that kind of thing. But you and I know what we're playing for."

"The cheering crowds and the pat on the back."

"And the Captain's smile as he says, 'Well done!' "

"That's it, Conway. That certainly is it."

"The Captain's words to the winning team," Conway went on, expanding again in anticipated glory. " 'Well played, sir, well played!' "

Then, suddenly abandoning his public declamation, Conway leaned forward confidentially, laid his hand on Willoughby's shoulder, and concluded in a stage whisper, "And the rotters and the bounders forever scrubbed out!"

Willoughby nodded. I began to think they were looking at me significantly out of their eye corners, and I turned away. I think I should have been able to forsake this tent without being addressed by anybody had it not been that, in turning rather hurriedly from Willoughby and Conway, I collided with another frock-coat.

"I'm terribly sorry," I said automatically, expecting a similar apology in reciprocation.

"That's quite all right," he said grandly, though in fact it was as much his fault as mine.

Now I have a secret admiration for the social accomplishment of being able, on the spur of the moment, to put the other fellow in the wrong; but it nettles me when exercised at my expense. Hence I was discomfited when he added, flicking his gloves over his feet,

"Don't worry: a little dust on the shoes; that's the only damage."

"Good," I said weakly, unable to prevent myself from aiding and abetting his assumption of superiority. He straightened himself and took my measure confidently.

"Were you looking for someone?" The tone implied that otherwise I ought not to be there.

"No," I said, already feeling unwanted.

"Is there something you want? Perhaps I can help you."

"No," I repeated, further flattened, "I just came in."

"You did," he said, with an assurance which shamed my ineffectiveness.

"And now I'm going out." My voice faltered noticeably.

"I'm glad to have met you, Mr. ...er...?"

Now this is one of the tricks I refuse to play up to. It has been worked on me once too often, and I know its effects. Whether the scene be a drawing-room or a street, it leaves you feeling like a candidate who is being interviewed for a job. So I dug my toes in.

"It's been a pleasure," I said.

There the first skirmish ended, and his manner changed.

"I say, were you thinking of joining us?"

"Not my line, I'm afraid."

"Oh, I'm sorry to hear that. Excuse my asking, old man, but what was your school?"

Brought up in a humble and unknown home of learning, I have had many years' experience of not answering this question.

"Little fame attaches to it," I said, "but it was effective in this instance."

He laughed.

"Oh, well, never mind. After all, we are going to the City. We shall all be equal there." This carried the implication that we were not yet equal here.

"I wish I could share your confidence on that point," I said. He nodded reflectively. The second skirmish ended and, after his fashion, he warmed.

"Look here, old man, I know your type, if you don't mind my saying so. In a sense you're educated. I mean, you've read books and that kind of thing. It does make a difference, even if you haven't mixed much. You'd fit in all right. You'd find the chaps here very decent."

I'm afraid I became very priggish.

"I've seen your preparations. And it seems to me that your people here have no notion of the seriousness of what you are embarking upon."

"Of course we haven't," he said frankly. "Have you?"

"Well, I admit that we're all groping in the dark. But everything that I associate with entry into the City—repentance and redemption and salvation— seems terribly remote from frock-coats, cricket bats and playing the game."

"It's the only code we really know. It has served us well: and, what is more important, we've tried to serve it." He spoke quite calmly and with no trace of sentiment or show. I nodded, feeling a trifle ashamed.

"It's a kind of symbolism," he went on, "and there's an awful lot involved in it—honesty, justice, courage, self-control, loyalty, service, and so on. Quite a string of virtues, when you come to think of it. I'm not saying the code is lived up to; but it *is* a code. There's the dim figure of a Captain too, upholding it all. Mind you, I'm not saying it's the stuff you get in church; but it's a damned good standard in its way. It has saved many a man from cowardice and many a woman from dishonour. Of course," he added as an afterthought, "any fool can make fun of it."

"Yes," I said. "It's a starting-point."

"And what has anyone got but that? We shall have to learn to give ourselves to something better; but we can't begin by wiping out what we've got that's good. We'd better serve that first."

The tables were turned. I was humbled—humbled before the absurdest terminology that ever diluted the ethos of Christendom. The code was not enough, yet I was not worthy to say so. These people were reliving the expression of the best earthly code they knew, intensified by a strange transfiguration, whilst I was reliving merely the dithers and hesitancies of inertia and indecision. Wouldn't it be far better to commit myself to a body—even a body so alien as this—than to go on, prying in rootless curiosity into the various modes of self-committal achieved by others? Who was I to go from one to the other of these committed and purposeful fellowships, passing judgment on their errors and inadequacies? My inconclusive wandering was itself becoming a torment.

"You will learn what you have chosen." Those were Manuel's words. And was this, then, what I had chosen—this role of the dilatory and critical outsider, isolated among the brotherly groups of pilgrims setting out for the Eternal City? And what was the alternative to further critical exploration? Must I choose between joining a parade of blimps in old school ties and taking part in a burlesque dramatisation of the *Canterbury Tales*? If only, if only I had joined that first procession, instead of clinging to Annot. I had thought it too stagey. But it was restrained, chaste and homely in comparison with what I had seen since. Indeed, there had been a congeniality about that first procession which I seemed every moment less and less likely to encounter again.

"I think we shall soon be on the move," said my companion, whose eyes had been wandering over the assembled groups. He nodded towards the far corner of the tent, and I followed his gaze.

Four of the women in gym-slips had hoisted on to their shoulders a contraption that looked like a stretcher. It was draped with a Union Jack. It supported a cushion, not unlike the cushion bearing the relics of Blessed Constance Wolfstone. But this cushion bore a large silver trophy. To my eyes, untrained in these mysteries, it looked uncommonly like the F.A. Cup; but presumably it had some other significance. At any rate, I saw that it was to be preceded in the procession by two of the athletic women, who carried upturned hockey-sticks before them, as an attendant chaplain might carry an episcopal crozier. This was enough for me.

"I'll be getting along," I said.

My companion nodded as if he understood.

"Good luck," he said. "We may meet again."

"Thanks," I muttered, and left the tent.

8

Upon one thing everyone here appears to be in agreement; that it is desirable to dress up in order to set out for Heaven. That was my first thought as I sampled the interior of a third marquee. For here the dominating atmosphere was puritanical and many of the costumed figures before me had a seventeenth-century appearance. Everywhere there were men in black cloaks, high-crowned felt hats, and plain buttoned doublets, whose general drabness was only accentuated by their broad square linen collars. I recalled portraits I had seen of seventeenth-century men of the Commonwealth: more particularly my mind went back to those dour Covenanters who march down from the Highlands in *Old Mortality* and lay siege to Tillietudlem. One group of sombre-suited gentlemen raised a smile immediately, for they looked like participants in a mass-stunt for advertising Quaker Oats. Adding a touch of variety to this rather chilling scene was a group of men and women dressed in grey uniforms. The men seemed to be members of some kind of religious "army": some of them carried instruments and obviously constituted a band. The women's uniform was less militaristic: they reminded me of deaconesses (C. of E.) in official attire: several of them carried black books: I thought they might well be a choir.

My interest in the scene was enlivened when I recognised among the bandsmen two of the instrumentalists who had led the procession out of Glenville. This discovery set me scanning the faces of the others to see whether the whole procession had come here. It was not easy to decide definitely about this. Dressing-up transforms people out of recognition sometimes, even when one knows them well, and I had merely caught a glimpse of the workers who left Glenville. Nevertheless I was sufficiently confident about the identity of one or two of the "puritans" to conjecture that the Glenville procession had come here in a body.

In assuring myself on this point, I stared too hard at a couple of men standing nearby, and they came to talk to me, surveying me at first with a somewhat stern and even suspicious air. The one was tall and lean, the other short and fat. I mention this because it gave them the appearance of specially chosen minor character actors in a comedy. Indeed, before they spoke, I had mentally associated them with Tribulation Wholesome (the fat one) and Ananias, his deacon, in Jonson's *Alchemist*. I'm afraid this irreverent imaginative identification of the two stuck in my mind and coloured our subsequent conversation.

"Friend, we have seen thee before," said Tribulation.

My first thought was of comic horror that I had encountered another bogus archaic lingo: but I responded politely.

"I was just thinking the same thing myself. I saw you in Glenville."

"We have forsaken the godless place and the adversaries of the Lord who dwell therein," said Tribulation.

"We have shaken the dust of it from our feet," echoed Ananias.

"I don't blame you," I said.

"It was a den of iniquity," said Tribulation.

"More abhorred than Sodom and Gomorrah," echoed Ananias.

"The Lord shall destroy it with a consuming fire," said Tribulation.

"With a mighty whirlwind shall He lay it low," added Ananias.

This sounded to me like a superfluous duplication of destructive agencies, ill-fitting the divine economy, but no doubt the biblical touch justified the repetition.

"It certainly was a hopeless place," I agreed, "really hopeless."

I tried to be as conversational as I could, hoping to ease the strain of their formal psalmody, for I was inwardly amused at the contrast between the plump stability of Tribulation, who stood with his feet planted wide apart on the ground, and the poker-faced frailty of Ananias, who moved gently from the waist upwards as he spoke. Tribulation might have been a rock and Ananias a tree swaying above him. Tribulation eyed me fixedly.

"Art thou numbered among the elect?"

Ananias's eyes rolled evasively as he made his addition.

"Is thy name written in the Book of Life?"

"I regret to say, gentlemen, that my personal salvation is a matter on which I have never been able to speak with confidence."

But Tribulation pushed on inexorably.

"If thou art washed in the Blood of the Lamb, thou art saved."

I couldn't very well disagree with this, so into the silence which followed I inserted a single monosyllable.

"Well?"

"Put off the garments of thy carnal days, and put on the new man in Christ."

"I simply can't understand," I said, "why it should be thought necessary to put on old-fashioned garments for the clothing of the new man."

"Oh," said Ananias, whining as though in pain, "my flesh is dried up like a potsherd and my belly cleaveth to the dust!"

This was, in part, an unexceptionable statement, for Ananias's flesh was indeed dried up. On the other hand, his belly was of such insignificant proportions that I could scarcely conceive it to be the cause of any major physiological disturbance within him.

Tribulation maintained his poise.

"These garments," he said, "belong to the days of thy wantonness in the lust of the flesh and the pride of life."

"Among them that go a-rioting and a-chambering," Ananias added.

"You may or may not have the right to judge me," I said, feigning annoyance,"but you certainly have no right to cast aspersions upon my friends and acquaintances. I lived in a highly respectable neighbourhood among people who had no vicious tendency in either of the two directions you mention. In point of fact, I think a bit of rioting might have been good for the place."

"This is the language of carnal jesting," said Tribulation.

"I take you for two broad-minded gentlemen," I

said ironically. "You appear to be uninhibited; for you are converting the pilgrimage to Heaven into a fancy-dress parade."

"Thou art a profane scoffer," Tribulation proclaimed. "Thou hast dwelt in the tents of the ungodly."

"Among the wine-bibbers and the whoremasters," added Ananias, apparently feeling the need to be more specific.

"There you go again, indulging in scandalous conjectures about the moral vagaries of my acquaintances, and all without the slightest foundation!"

"Idle mockery," said Tribulation quietly, but Ananias responded less calmly.

"I am poured out like water," he groaned, swaying with an almost liquid flexibility, "and all my bones are out of joint."

It seemed to me highly ridiculous that a man of Ananias's spare and extenuated physique should have accustomed himself to the use of these physiological metaphors, but I suppressed comment and Tribulation seemed to melt a little.

"Brother, what hinders thee from joining us?"

"Your clothes, for one thing."

"There are deeper hindrances than that."

"Yes," I said, "I think there are. I have more sympathy with those who follow the relics of Blessed Constance Wolfstone; the knights and burgesses and vested priests."

"They bow down to graven images," said Tribulation, "and burn that incense which is an abomination unto the Lord."

"It stinketh in His nostrils," said Ananias.

"That's what it's meant to do," I said.

"They deck themselves in purple and gold," said Tribulation.

"It's as becoming as black and white."

"And behold," said Ananias, "they that wear fine raiment are in kings' houses."

"That's where they are going; to the King's House." Tribulation nodded gravely.

"Thou has determined to join them?"

"No," I said, falling into his idiom, "I'm tarrying the Lord's leisure."

"The Bridegroom cometh. Beware lest thou tarriest too long, and be numbered among the foolish virgins."

"That would be a pleasant change," I said, "after being classed with the whoremongers."

"Thou art given over to fond raillery," said Tribulation.

"A mocker and a blasphemer," said Ananias, "whose throat is an open sepulchre."

Coming from a man whose cavernous mouth hung suspended above an elongated neck, this comment was a fitting conclusion: and there was a smile on my lips as they turned away in solemn displeasure. Then I suddenly jumped nervously to a tap on my shoulder and the words of a voice behind me.

"Were you quite fair?"

I turned quickly to face an obviously clerical figure, wearing a cassock and a graduate gown. He was an oldish, thin-faced individual with grey hair and bushy eyebrows, whose eyes had a critical keenness.

"Stubbs is the name. Dr. Stubbs, to be precise."

"How do you do," I said.

He shook his head in a gesture of rebuke.

"Any fool can bait the puritanical."

"They asked for it," I said, embarrassed none the less.

"Did they?"

There was an awkward pause. I shrugged my shoulders.

"All that about wine-bibbing and whoring," I said.

"Were you really so unintelligent as to take their rhetorical metaphors literally? Or did you perhaps think it was a good game?"

"I enjoyed it," I admitted.

"So did I."

"And I don't think it did them any harm."

"None at all. It probably did them good. But how you damaged yourself!"

"Oh," I said, nonplussed.

"They invited you to join us."

"And I refused."

"First, on grounds of costume."

"I'm not going to argue about that," I said. "I've already had dressing-up fully explained to me by an argument which I've forgotten. But I remember that it justified any kind of sartorial extravagance in those setting out for the City."

"Good. Then we can leave that question aside. What else made you find them absurd?"

"They weren't absurd. At least Tribulation wasn't. You will admit that Ananias has an amusing appearance."

"Why 'Tribulation' and 'Ananias'? These are not their names."

I explained carefully.

"They reminded me straight away of Ben Jonson."

"Ah. You decided from the start that they were comic characters."

I couldn't deny this and I felt rather ashamed.

"And yet, had you been differently disposed, they might have reminded you, instead, of sober-suited figures from history, not from stage comedy—John Bunyan perhaps, or John Milton."

"I didn't recognise a Miltonic ring when they spoke, nor even the accents of Bunyan."

"You're trying to be clever again. They are both simple unlettered people: yet the Johns might have recognised them as of their own tradition."

"Maybe."

"So that this biblical idiom could scarcely of itself be a reason for rejecting their invitation."

"One moment," I said. "Much as I admire Milton, I don't think I should have found myself at his side in public worship."

"But you would not have tried to be clever at his expense?"

The very notion was enough to make a man quail in his boots.

"Of course not," Dr. Stubbs went on, answering the question for me. "I'm only trying to make a single point. If you are going to judge a given Christian tradition, you'd better judge it at its best. Otherwise you will get nowhere. I mention this because it seems to me, from what I have heard, that you are just now busily occupied in getting nowhere."

"You're right," I said, and waited for more.

"If you don't follow this advice, you will find that you are merely judging irrelevancies. You will think you have come up against a corrupt tradition or an erroneous community, when you have merely met with an individual less intelligent or less informed than yourself."

"Yes," I said. "I can see the difference."

"For you it's a crucial difference. Suppose you meet Mr. X, who says he's a logical positivist, and then you discover that he beats his wife. You would be wrong to conclude that the philosophy of logical positivism involves wife-beating as one of its tenets. Again, suppose you meet Mr. Y, who claims to be a Moravian, and then reveals himself to be in the habit of gossiping scandalously about his acquaintances. You would be wrong to pronounce Moravianism a religion of malice. I will give you one more example. Suppose you meet Mr. Z, who is a vegetarian and cannot sing in tune. It would be fallacious to conclude that vegetarianism precludes a developed aesthetic sensibility."

"I've got the point," I said, a little wearily, feeling that he drove it home once too often.

"I have made three distinct points, not one. The first is this. You must not judge a code on irrelevancies which fall outside the scope of its jurisdiction. The second is this. You must not judge a code by the moral failing of its weaker adherents. The third is this. You must not judge a code by the intellectual and cultural limitations of its less educated supporters. For the word *code* you may substitute the word *religion*, or even the word *denomination*."

"I understand that," I said, getting slightly irritated by his precise instructive manner.

"Now," he went on, "you have gone from tent to tent, seeking a body of worshippers congenial enough for you to join them."

"That is so. And I've been disappointed so far."

"Because you are continually meeting with a Mr. X, a Mr. Y, or a Mr. Z."

"I have also had some communication with Messrs. A, B, and C."

"Maybe; but in spite of the rational appeal of what they said, you have come away from each tent more under the influence of your emotional response to their less representative fellows."

There was some truth in this. I had to admit to myself that I had not been put off by what Father Thomas had said, nor by what the communicative frock-coat had said. Rather I had been attracted to them. And it was the same with Dr. Stubbs. Something was attracting me to *every* company, just as surely as something was repelling me from each. Was everything that repelled a mere negative personal deviation, and everything that attracted a part of the true faith of partially failing individuals? If this were the case, every failure to be attracted in sympathy was a failure of will and judgment on my part, a failure to clear the mind of confusion and to cleanse the heart of moral arrogance. I judged myself in judging others. Every admission that I was repelled was a confession that I had failed in mental grip or in moral integrity. But, if this were true, how could I ever choose between the diverse groups? The very basis of judging between them seemed to have been obliterated by logic and morality. All, as the latitudinarians would say, were really the same. And this was a conclusion which I could not accept; for it seemed to destroy objectivity.

"You are right," I said. "But I'm by no means sure what follows. What must I do?"

"You must destroy the self which impedes your progress, bogging you down in indecision. You must be converted by death of the old Adam, and accept salvation freely offered in the living power of the Resurrection."

"That doesn't settle my doubts."

"The Blood of Christ atones."

"But I don't know which body to join. There are difficulties."

"They are the difficulties of the old Adam. He is to die."

"Not wholly so. They are also the searchings of my God-given reason."

"Faith alone saves. Your reason is corrupt."

"Corrupted perhaps; not in itself corrupt."

"Ah!" He nodded as if in acceptance of some new illumination.

"I know the answer," I said. "I was told it often enough on earth. I must seek the shelter of the Church's discipline, intellectual as well as spiritual. But that, oddly enough, is what I have not been able to find here."

"Perhaps you weren't really seeking it."

"Perhaps not," I said, feeling as far away as ever.

"But you have given me the answer I sought," he said, rather sadly. "It is now plain as a pikestaff what you ought to do."

"Then tell me," I said eagerly.

"You seek the discipline of an authoritative Body, to sustain your faith with dogma and to feed your spirit with the nourishment of the altar. You have lived on earth reinforced by hierarchy and sacrament. You must go immediately."

"Where?"

"Back straight away to *Ad Sanctam Civitatem*, to join the company to whom you belong."

"To play my part in a pseudo-mediaeval pageant and to talk like *Stories of Robin Hood?*" I protested.

"These are irrelevancies. The weaknesses of Messrs. X, Y, and Z. There is no time to lose."

He bundled me out of the tent, so unsure of myself that I did indeed act under the compulsion of his influence. Outside the tent it was strangely quiet and I made my way slowly along the edge of the field to the first marquee, whose entrance faced the drive from the Highway. Lost in doubt whether I was acting or merely being acted upon, I approached the tent as one might walk towards a funeral, and I was too moody and disconcerted to register any clear impressions as I sauntered reluctantly inside.

The scene that greeted me within was all the greater shock. It was a double shock—a shock of surprise, and a shock of realisation, for now at last I knew what I wanted, when it was too late to claim it. The place was utterly deserted. They had gone; copes, candles, censers and crucifixes; the relics of the Blessed Constance Wolfstone; the bright medley of rich tunics, cloaks and headgear; the solemn array of cottas, albs and religious habits; the heralds, the pennants, the trumpets and the spears; all departed to leave the place as bare and desolate as the grave. I felt that nothing would be too dear a price for the purchase of a single breath of incense, a single rustle of silk, a single phoney "Gadzooks." But they had gone their ways, playing their magnificent, courtly and preposterous game as citizens of the dreamed-of theocentric State; vaunting their pennants, riding their palfreys, talking of jousts and lutes and ladies' bowers, they exalted themselves in their high unhistoric drama and made their final pilgrimage behind the sacred relics and the uplifted cross to the high unhistoric City of God.

And I might have been with them. That was the bitterness. I turned disconsolately from the depressing emptiness and left the tent. Then I saw something which had escaped my notice on entry. Two men had removed the banner *Ad Sanctam Civitatem* and were replacing it by another which read, *No tribunal but the Word of Life: No confessional but the Throne of Grace*. It appeared that a quite different gathering was being prepared for.

Lacking any clear intention in my dejection, I walked from the field, down the drive towards the Highway. I passed John Bunyan's wicket gate and soon came in sight of the road. When I actually reached it, the clerk in the wooden enquiry office called me through his open window and then came running out to talk to me.

"You're not going away?" He sounded incredulous.

"I was thinking of it."

"We never disappoint clients, never. How many tents have you sampled?"

"Three."

"Not enough," he said decisively. "What put you off?"

"Distracting irrelevancies, I'm afraid: like fancy dress."

"I see," he said, surveying me thoughtfully. "I think I know your type. We can fix you up if you give us the chance. Let me try."

He was courteous and well-meaning and I had no definite aim, so I allowed him to lead me back into the field. We walked right around the edge to the far side, which I had not inspected, and he directed me to a smaller marquee than those I had already sampled. It looked very cosy, sheltering between larger tents.

"This may be just the ticket," the clerk said. "And if it isn't, there's no need to despair. We have lots more. I'll leave you here. I mustn't neglect the office too long."

9

Certainly this tent was different. Being smaller it seemed less awesome, and being occupied by only a handful of people it had a more restful air. Several things contributed to this air of greater restfulness. For instance, although I had seen one or two older persons sitting on folding canvas chairs of the highback variety, by far the majority of the people in the other tents had been standing about in groups. Here, however, all were sitting—perhaps one should say lying—in deckchairs. Moreover, they were all men, and I missed immediately that background of high-pitched feminine voices, suitably restrained yet insistent, against which we had chatted in the other marquees. Lastly, these men were in ordinary twentieth-century dress, and pretty informal dress too—mostly grey flannels and sportsjackets, tweeds or corduroys.

There was no banner, no fancy dress, no paraphernalia and, in short, no fuss. The men lounged lazily, their deck-chairs disposed in little groups. They chatted quietly, waved their hands occasionally in illustrative gesture, and pulled intermittently at their cigarettes. Yes, that was another difference. Here sev-

116

eral of the men were smoking. One or two had books or magazines on their laps, but there was nothing else about. Now although this tent spoke a greater reposefulness, it was not an immediately comfortable place to enter; less so, in fact, than the others. There the large crowds, the standing groups and the general air of busyness had enabled me for much of the time to play the part of an unobserved spectator. Here, on the other hand, it was impossible to get lost in the throng and to preserve one's anonymity. Standing inside the entrance, I was immediately aware of myself as an intruder.

No one rose or came forward to greet me, but a man nearby nodded towards me and then significantly kicked a vacant chair which stood within his reach. Thus informally welcomed, I gathered that I was expected to join his little group and I readily took the hint. The gentleman who had thus warmly drawn me in was a slim, angular-faced individual, half of whose jacket was crumpled up between his shoulders and his thick, wiry hair as he gazed restfully at the roof of the tent. He addressed his two companions with considerable fervour and assurance.

"She was a lovely job, with a body that curved like a waterfall. Sleek as a greyhound she was. Made you proud to be seen out with her. Quite the nicest piece of work I ever came across, and sound as a bell. I ought to know: I stripped her down often enough."

A little shocked, I prepared myself for the confessions of a philanderer. But I soon discovered my mistake.

"I once took her for a tour of Scotland. Three thousand miles in a fortnight. The hills and the rush would have torn the guts out of any ordinary model, you'd have said. But she went like a dream: never murmured. I didn't open the bonnet the whole fortnight except to top up the oil and water. She'd have converted you, Tom."

Apparently Tom was the name of the large gentleman on my left, for he shook his head incredulously as one not given to rapid conversions. Such was his build that even this slight movement appeared to be achieved only at the cost of considerable physical strain. Dark-suited and black-haired, he was the smooth type, with a complexion like dough and two tired eyes. Even his speech came in jerks, as though he was permanently out of breath.

"Never got on with small cars. Don't know why. Never did. Some people don't. Some people do. Not me. Always had a Daimler." The grammatical ellipses suggested a long-ingrained habit of economising to the maximum in the expenditure of effort.

"I'm ready to take a bet," the first continued, "I could have left you standing on the open road and still have had plenty to spare."

"Never thought they paid, small cars," Tom puffed. "Buy quality. In for a penny, in for a pound. Pays in the long run."

"She was an exception, a lucky fluke, wasn't she, Bert?"

"Jim's quite right. She was a car in a thousand." Bert was a placid, amiable-looking creature, with a bright bespectacled face and thinning hair. His light-coloured voice expressed a personality altogether less assertive than those of his companions.

"It isn't what you pay for a car," said Jim decisively. "It's how you treat her. You've got to know her inside out. Respect her little weaknesses, and don't force her."

The trio bored me. I am ready to indulge in small talk when the occasion seems to require it. I am happy to discuss brands of tobacco or of razor-blades with any intelligent connoisseur; but I have always understood it to be the worst possible form to expatiate in company about cars or golf. Moreover, I was rather appalled. No one else I had met in the Border Country had discussed such mundane trivialities. The contrast between the zealous pieties I had encountered in the evangelical convention and this abysmally earthly obsession was quite shocking. I felt it my duty to twist the conversation.

"Do you really think this talk appropriate? You are on the way to Heaven; and you're not going to drive there."

Tom grunted, Bert smiled and Jim looked bored. It was plain that Heaven would have been a more attractive proposition in their eyes, could they have completed their pilgrimage by means of the internal combustion engine.

"Consider your situation," I exhorted them, "and the road that lies before you."

"From what I've seen," said Jim, brightening, "it's got the surface of an unclassified cart-track."

"No good for speed," said Tom. "Ought to be widened. Death-traps at every bend. Pot-holes, too."

"This is not an earthly road," I said, "it's a heavenly one."

"Not my idea of a heavenly road," said Jim.

"Hellish for springs," said Tom.

"And for tires," said Bert.

"What's the use," said Jim, with considerable feeling, "what's the use of putting your brains into devel-
oping a really delicate front-wheel suspension, when
they leave tracks like that about the place?"

"Gentlemen," I protested, breaking in again. "This
is most improper. There are graver things to ponder
here. You sit back talking about springs and front-
wheel suspension, when you have the most solemn
journey you ever undertook ahead of you. Surely it's
time to think about starting."

"I don't have the slightest trouble with it," said Jim,
"even in winter. I flood the carburetor, swing the handle three times with the ignition off, switch on, touch
the button, and she sings like a bird."

"Never used a handle," said Tom. "Never needed
one. Never possessed one. Just press. That's all. Off
she goes."

"You're obsessed, gentlemen," I cried, "obsessed! If
there were a single spark of spirituality in you, you
wouldn't be able to sit here and revolve such appalling
trivialities. But there isn't. Not a spark."

"Ignition trouble," said Jim. "Ten to one the plugs
want cleaning."

"Battery dead," said Tom.

I rose from my seat in disgust and walked away
without another word. My intention was to leave the
marquee, but a newly-placed obstacle lay between
myself and the entrance—two deck-chairs, one vacant, the other occupied by an earnest-looking individual considerably my senior, who seemed to be
waiting for me. At any rate, he motioned to me to sit
in the empty chair and then placed his hands together
over a book on his lap, as if he meant to talk at leisure.

"My names is Miles," he said.

I introduced myself.

"You are surprised at what you find here?"

"Astonished," I said.

He nodded, crossed his legs and began to swing his foot.

"This tent is different. For one thing, it's new: added very recently and set apart for a purpose which none of the others serves."

I listened in silence and he warmed to his subject.

"As a matter of fact, I was personally responsible for its erection and opening. I'm not a boastful man, but I think I can claim to have effected a minor revolution in this camping ground. We offer here something which no other group ever thought of offering."

He waited for comment, but I continued silent.

"You've seen something of the other marquees?"

I nodded.

"When I first came," he went on, "I investigated every one of them. There was none that satisfied me. They were all equally at fault. I detected two major evils in the attitude of every group I contacted; a fundamental flippancy and a gross insincerity."

"That's putting it very strongly," I protested.

"It is justified. The flippancy is manifested in the universal habit of dressing up. They treat the very serious matter of pilgrimage to Heaven as an opportunity for playing an elaborate charade. The insincerity is revealed in the general tendency to adopt a fashion of speech and bearing quite foreign to the earthly dispositions of the pilgrims. I thought things over carefully, and I made my great decision. It shall be my business, I said, to revolutionise the human approach to Heaven, to cleanse it of play, fantasy and pretence. There shall be a new group, and the keynotes of their pilgrimage shall be simplicity and sincerity."

There was some sense in this and I nodded appreciatively.

"I knew there must be many who felt as I did," he continued, "and I was determined to cater for them. It wasn't easy, but the long and short of it is that I got the permission of the Trust, who added this small tent and promised to erect a full-sized one if the numbers I gathered should justify it. So this new department is operating under my chosen conditions. No trappings, no ceremonial, no dressing-up, no false courtesies, no artificial etiquettes, no high-falutin speech. I am catering for simple men who want to be themselves, men who want to enter the City, not as dramatised personalities, but as their genuine familiar selves. If you want to carry on the road a dressed-up doll, you'll find the chance to do so in any other group on the field. But if you want to take to the City your own congenial earthly self, this is the place for you—and it's the only place. We have set our faces against pretence."

Miles had a convincing utterance and a tranquil but confident manner. I was interested to see that he didn't actively press me to join his group. He merely stated their aims and conditions. This was rational and just. On the other hand, his sane explanation accorded ill with the puerile trivialities I had already met with in the tent. I nodded towards the trio.

"Their interests are very limited," I said, "Jim and Tom, I think they're called."

"Jim Wheeler and Tom Wheeler. They are brothers; and their cousin Bert." He smiled. "We call them the Three Wheelers."

"Very appropriate. They are scarcely ripe for the City."

"That's where you are wrong," he said earnestly. "They have fitted in admirably. Some of those who join us prove much more difficult to discipline than our friends here. They all come with the right aim, of course, but too many of them continue to hanker after dressing up, putting on a role, forsaking their real selves. Something in the very atmosphere of the Border Country seems to infect them with this cursed passion for doing an act. It is often quite difficult to confine their wayward aspirations within the honest aim of being true to themselves. The Three Wheelers have not been difficult. I admit, as you say, that their interests are limited; but this has made it all the easier to save them from pretence and insincerity. They have never sought to adopt false roles. They are simple, honest souls, prepared to take their unsullied ingenuous selves to the City. There'll be no nonsense when they first shake hands with God. No bowing and scraping; no thee and thou; but an honest straightforward 'How do you do.' That's the kind of men they are; the pure in heart, who have become as little children. And that's as it should be. J.C. was quite right."

These informal references to God and to Our Lord jarred in my ears. Indeed these few words suddenly transformed my whole attitude to Miles. This was because a distant memory came back to me from an extraordinary experience of long ago, and the wise words of a friend and guide rang in my head. "How would you distinguish a true servant of God from a traitor?...You should take especial notice how a person speaks, not of other things, but of God." Here there was neither reverence nor humility. In a flash the whole fraud stood revealed for what it was.

"You've given the show away," I said, "just when it was beginning to take me in."

"There's no attempt here to take anybody in."

"Oh, yes, there is. The whole thing is a deception. You think you're merely restraining people from dressing up: but in fact you're frustrating the making of new men. You think you're saving people from pretence, when you're engaged in trying to cancel out redemption and obliterate regeneration. That's what it is. You're trying to pin human souls down eternally in their natural earthly selfhood. Can't you see what you're doing to these people? The things you are denying them—new speech, new dress, high ceremony and courtesy—are the means of worship, transfiguration and self-transcendence. You're locking them up in their petty sensual limitations. Why, it's better to dance to Heaven in a riotous carnival of mummers than to drag along the slouching untransfigured self with its hands in its earthly pockets. Better a million mass-produced rosaries and a vulgar, tawdry little statue of the Sacred Heart in everyone's hands, than this everlasting earthbound chatter about carburetors and miles per gallon."

I chose my rhetorical examples with intent to irritate, but Miles remained calm.

"We have no use for superstitious tokens and observances of any kind. They shroud the pure, naked personality in a veil of misty dreams and unrealities. We shall remain true to ourselves and eschew every technique of self-deception. By rituals and false idolatries men deceive themselves into believing they are other than they know themselves at heart to be. They dress

up, strut around and pompously talk themselves into
fantasy roles. They really come to believe in the fanta-
sies they have created, imagining themselves armed
knights or aristocratic gents or puritan evangelists.
And in this fantasy condition they will attach significance to any ridiculous token or grimace. The pure
spirituality of man is whittled away in a bogus pantomime. It's revolting. Man loses his stark genuine humanity and is transformed into a vulgar puppet. He
becomes a living lie."

I stood up and went through all the motions of being outraged.

"What astonishes me is to hear this stuff from someone on the borders of Heaven. For I've heard it all before—or something very like it. Only that was on the
borders of Hell."

"You've travelled widely," he said slyly.

"Widely enough to know what belongs to Hell."

"I'm sorry not to have had the same advantages myself."

"Don't worry," I said. "You will."

After that I left him, thoroughly disgusted both
with him and with myself. With him because of the
pernicious nonsense he talked: with myself because he
had almost taken me in, and because I had given such
a priggish display of bad temper. I knew his scheme
was damnable and deserved everything I had said of
it. But my being in the right brought neither comfort
nor peace. In some paradoxical way it put me more
hopelessly in the wrong. For the more I searched this
encampment, the deeper I seemed to be submerged in
the character of a self-righteous critic. One or two saving moments apart, my whole course in this wretched

field had been a career of passing judgment on others. Could that be what I was called to do? Manuel had told me that I should discover what I had chosen. If he was right—as of course he must be—then I had chosen the role of outsider and self-righteous critic.

Yet I was right to judge Miles's scheme harshly. Wherein then did my wrongness lie? Here was a subtle problem. Partly, no doubt, it lay in the emotional quality and moral background of my outbursts—the malice and vanity which accompanied them. But there seemed to be much more to it than that. Maybe the wrongness lay in my being there at all. Yet the visit had done me good in many ways, if only in teaching me what I had chosen and failed to choose. In that sense, my being there was good. Why, then, was I burdened with such a weight of guilt that I felt increasingly wrong in my very acts of rightness?

Illumination came to me in a flash. The fundamental wrongness lay in my being myself. What an obvious corollary it was. For the fundamental rightness of those who had marched off to the City in pseudo-mediaeval splendour lay precisely in this—that they were trying to transcend themselves. Miles and his group, on the other hand, were insisting on being themselves. Which was my own error. Small wonder that I attacked it with such vehemence. I was attacking the venom in myself. And small wonder that I was guilty in the very act of condemning it. It was a double guilt. The guilt of sharing Miles's guilt, and the guilt of condemning in others the guilt I shared.

I had walked round the edge of the field to the end of the drive again. And this time I really determined to leave the place. I shall inspect no more tents, I said. As a visiting inspector I've finished. If I've learned nothing else, I've learned this; that I must drop the role of external examiner. So I walked down the drive and concentrated on the immediate practical problem of how to get past the clerk in the enquiry bureau without any embarrassing discussion. When I got there, it proved easy. A small group of new arrivals was gathered round the hut. I couldn't even see the clerk's face.

I turned right along the Highway and proceeded alone.

10

At first it was a relief to be away from the crowds, but soon I began to feel lonely. I wished I could have found some happy mean between the throng of the encampment and the solitude of the road. One of the surprising qualities of the Border Country was the absence of such happy means. Whilst I trod the Highway I seemed, for the most part, to be on a lonely disused road; but whenever I deviated a little, I encountered considerable numbers of people, in one way or another engaged upon the same journey as myself.

The contrast between the solitariness and the crowds was of a piece with the sharply accentuated distinctions which had impressed me from the start. It was also in accord with the sequence of incongruities which constituted my pilgrimage. Among these incongruities was the odd mixture of the rural and the urban. I do not mean that I ever came to anything like an earthly township; but from time to time my progress along this peaceful lane was varied by strange reminders of what we call "civilisation."

For instance, a road sign gave a surprising introduction to the downward slope ahead of me.

THE VALLEY OF DESOLATION
Pilgrims are warned not to loiter or linger.

The district did not look in the least desolate. I made a quite romantic descent through a winding avenue overhung at each side by a single line of trees. The country was clear and unshadowed at the bottom of the hill, where the lane bent sharply to the left over a stone bridge. Then another of those sudden incongruities. To the right a much wider road swept up to iron gates surmounted by the announcement,

AYENBITE OF INWIT
The House of Remorse.

I did not forget the warning at the top of the hill when I turned into this entrance: rather I assumed that it could not possibly apply to anything so disciplined as the pursuit of remorse. The announcement seemed to promise the reverse of temptation and indulgence, and it was scarcely likely to appeal to the self-satisfied. So I followed the drive without questioning that I did the right thing. It narrowed quickly to a second entrance which consisted of a single turnstile. I wondered what the point of this could be, since no one was in attendance. The notice at its side—SINNERS THIS WAY—scarcely suggested that entertainment was to be had within. The mechanism clicked as I went through. No doubt it was some device for numbering the sinners. I was too stupid to realise that it allowed ingress but not egress.

Eventually I came upon signs of life. Two men stood before the door of a little stone building. As I approached, an attendant gave something to each of them and they moved off. Then came the shock of as-

tonishment. What I saw seemed to be the very epitome of irreverence, triviality and worldliness. My two
predecessors advanced towards a semi-circle of unnameable machines and proceeded to operate two of
them. To all appearances they were nothing more or
less than those machines one sees on the pier at the
more vulgar seaside resorts and in the seedier corners
of amusement grounds. They invite you to be a spectator of what the butler or the window-cleaner saw.
What extraordinary purgatorial device was this?
Whatever were these people looking at? I must confess
that my earthbound mind toyed briefly with the absurd notion that biblical instruction was perhaps being offered in visual form under such titles as
Susannah and the Elders or *The Dance of Salome*.

"Do you want a film?"

The voice of the attendant startled me.

"Of what?" I asked automatically. I hope I wasn't
secretly hoping for an eyebrow-raiser.

"Of your past life. That's the only kind of film we
have here."

"I didn't know you had that. I'd no idea my life had
been filmed."

He chuckled.

"There are lots of things you've no idea of yet.
We've got films of everybody's life. Not complete, of
course. You wouldn't expect that. But enough to give a
general idea."

Before I could reply, he disappeared into his little
room and emerged soon after with a little cardboard
box inscribed with my name.

"Pop it in the machine. There's a little socket at the
left-hand side."

"Thank you," I said, and lingered.

"Now don't tell me you don't know how to work one of these machines," he said slyly.

"Well," I said, evasively, "I'm not very mechanically-minded."

"You don't need to be. These things aren't designed for the mechanically-minded. Ordinary human instincts will see you through."

I began to move off.

"Sorry I can't supply you with an early Dietrich."

"It would leave me cold," I said scornfully.

"Well, this won't. It'll rock you."

Thus forewarned, I chose a lonely stance at the farthest end of the row of machines from my two predecessors, inserted my film and began to turn the handle. Before I saw anything at all I was disquieted by a sense of shame and indignity. Had I come, then, to the Borderlands of Heaven to spend my time in a side-show? Could the content of the film possibly justify my being in the position of a Peeping Tom? I had a quite irrational impulse to look round and see whether anyone was watching me at my humiliating occupation; but curiosity soon swamped any desire to withdraw.

NOSCE TEIPSUM
(Know thyself)
Visual Aids to Repentance
Guaranteed to stir the stubbornest
heart and will.
Photography and Commentary by
MORAL MOVIES Ltd.

O LORD, Thou hast searched me
out and known me.
THOU hast
condemned all mine iniquities
and
Thanks to MORAL MOVIES Ltd.
I can see what You're getting at.

YOU shall see yourself as others
see you.
YOU shall observe
the severed identities of your
SPIRITUAL and NATURAL selves.

After this third caption the photography began. I was presented with myself in duplicate. I was walking about the home and garden I had so recently left behind. But there were two of me, separated by inches only and going through identical movements in opening doors, climbing steps, treading the lawn, examining the roses and so on. This effect might have been achieved by a trick technique of earthly photography, had the two selves been wholly identical in appearance as well as in movement; but they weren't. The foremost figure had more than a touch of caricature. The lips were lustfully thickened and loosened, the slight slope of the my mouth exaggerated so as to appear malicious and supercilious, the eyes pushed more closely under the eyebrows so as to suggest stupidity and bad temper. Moreover the arms were slightly lengthened and the hands subtly enlarged, and this gave a frightening impression of greed and grasping covetousness. In the same way a slight enlargement of the lower legs and feet made me look a thorough clod. Plainly this was my natural self, and its grossness was a compound of sensuality, stupidity and untamed boorishness. It was utterly repellent.

Behind this unattractive creature my spiritual self moved in mimicry. It was me all right, but subtle touches had ironed out physical discordances of feature and figure, producing a harmony of just proportions without damaging the true personal distinctiveness. It was the kind of idealised study which an expensive West End photographer might have produced, with the help of consummate artistry, had my publishers been called upon, by the clamour of the public, to produce for their benefit The Man Behind the Book.

I must make it quite clear that, in spite of the handsome physical proportions, my spiritual self did not attract me in the least. It had an ethereal quality about the eyes and a simpering piety about the mouth which seemed to me regrettably affected. Repelled as I was by the earthiness of Natural me, I could yet find no comfort in studying the handsome, clear-eyed transparency of Spiritual me. With all its gracefulness, it looked hypocritical.

YOU have seen yourself
on earth.
NOW see yourself
on your final pilgrimage.

My two selves were sitting with Annot at the side of the Highway. Natural I was leering at my companion and the large hands pawed the outline of her body without actually touching it. Spiritual I gazed in exaggerated rapture at the procession of pilgrims just passing before us. Natural I turned to grimace and gesture scornfully at the procession. Spiritual I stood up and moved towards the pilgrims, looking like a Hollywood actor being holy in a religious film. Immediately Natural I got up, took from its pocket a book labelled EXCUSES, tapped Spiritual me on the shoulder and drew attention to the contents of the volume. Sadly, Spiritual I returned to the roadside with Natural me, the latter grinning in triumph.

It was a ludicrous pantomime, and for a moment I stopped winding to ask myself whether it was intellectually—or even morally—justifiable to continue the grotesque performance. The burlesque character of the thing shocked me: so did the vulgar character of Spiritual me's role. If this were a just representation of myself, then my spiritual impulses were as contemptible as my crudest earthly desires. They were all equally self-centered, the supernatural impulses as rotten with hypocritical vanity as my worldly desires were corrupt with sensuality. Was this what I was meant to learn? Contempt for every impulse within me that had ever emerged on the surface in word or action? Despair of ever disentangling a single movement of my heart from its roots in utter vanity and sensuality?

An intriguing caption had replaced the latest sequence of photographs.

HOW IT ALL BEGAN
YOU started your life
as a child of God.

I saw my mother wheeling a pram away from the church in which I was baptised. My father was at her side with my elder brother in a sailor suit. My uncles and aunts followed in clothes which must have been out-of-date even at that time, during the First World War. I glued my eyes upon my baby self. The appearance was comic and yet blasphemous too. For my head, raised on the pillow, was two years older than the rest of the infant body, and the face beamed with a devastatingly self-satisfied innocence. Worst of all, the head was surrounded by a halo!

I had scarcely digested this when another caption succeeded.

THE damage is done.

Here was I, curly-haired and plump, at the age of about six. And there was still only one of me. Moreover, I was still wearing the halo. I stood in the middle of the drawing room in the first home I knew, surrounded by relations. It was obvious that I was the centre of admiration. Uncle Stephen was rocking with laughter and slapping his great knees with his hands. Aunt Susan's arms were held aloft in mock astonishment. Great Aunt May was nodding her head knowingly in unmistakable approval of myself. And Father and Mother beamed proudly upon actor and audience in this little silent drama. Suddenly everybody started to nod their heads violently as if in agreement with some new suggestion. My father approached me and laid his hand on my shoulder. The film director had recourse to a caption again.

"GO through your recitation
again, Sonny, for your
aunts and uncles."

Back to photography, and to me at six years mouthing inaudible verses, plainly rather proud of myself. The camera gave a short sample of my performance.

"IT was the schooner *Hesperus*
That sailed the wintry sea,
And the skipper had taken his little
daughter
To bear him company."

No more was quoted. The banal verses had to be imagined as my little image mouthed and gestured before the delighted company. But as the increasing vehemence of my stilted infantile movements began to suggest the tragic unfolding of the tale, an extraordinary thing happened. The halo around my curly head began to rise gradually, detaching itself from me, and coming to rest above my head. Then, as it hung in the air, suspended like the full moon, it began to increase in size until it was bigger than the child it overhung. Nor was this the end of its transmutations, for it now began to assume an additional dimension, swelling by degrees until it was spherical instead of circular. There it hung, like a giant orange, its skin bulging here and there as if it were going to burst. At this point my performance of the poem ended and the relations began to clap. I gazed around in childish triumph. Then it happened. The suspended orange did indeed burst and gave forth a shower of sparks like a ball thrown up from a Roman Candle. In bursting it deposited its contents at my side—a second self, identical in outline and as yet indistinguishable in feature. The two of me joined hands and scampered from the assembled company. The halo was gone forever.

This was farcical. There was no other word for it. I stopped winding and tried to laugh. But I couldn't. For the farce had a horrible meaningfulness that stung me bitterly. I knew that it was only the visual technique which was laughable—the grotesque exaggeration, the ludicrous concretion of the unseeable and the intangible. It was all right for detached spectators to laugh at this kind of thing. It was like laughing at an absurdly vicious personification in a Morality Play. But this ridiculous victim of film allegory was me! Here was lost an integrity never yet regained. Here was the beginning of a vain self-centredness which had severed me from my spiritual roots and left me, quite literally, a creature of duplicity.

I forsook the wretched machine, convinced that the film could tell me no more. I had seen the end and the beginning. It was not difficult to imagine what came in between. But the picturing of it, in this astonishing idiom, was more than I could bear. All the devices of sharp exaggeration and farcical concretion had been exploited to the end of making my moral career, not merely shameful, but ridiculous too. I was contemptible. I had said so a thousand times in psalms and prayers, but I had never really known what it meant. Now I knew indeed, tasted the full flavour of that compound of the shameful and the farcical which the idea of the contemptible comprehends. Of course I had always known intellectually that sin was absurd as well as wicked. The absurdity of sin had been a notion familiar to me in my amateurish philosophising. But to see this abstraction, absurdity, concretely realised in relation to my own personal sinfulness induced an emotional disturbance shocking in its intensity.

I saw that one of my predecessors had been overcome like myself. He had withdrawn from his machine and he stood with shaking shoulders, obviously weeping. I went over to him, glad to encounter a fellow sufferer. He wiped his eyes.

"You've no idea what I've seen," he said. "I expect it's the worst thing they've ever had to film."

"I'm ready to dispute that," I said.

"No, no. Mine's the worst. It's an all-time low. I'm the dregs. You can't imagine."

"I can," I assured him, "only too well."

"No, you can't. I'm the scum. I'm a disgrace to my name."

"What *is* your name?"

"Smith," he said tragically. "That's my name. It was my father's name too. And I'm not worthy of it."

"I think you and I feel pretty much the same," I said

encouragingly. "I know I'm a worm."

"Worms crawl," he said. "I'm not fit to crawl."

There seemed to be no answer to this. Whatever else, Smith was certainly not going to relinquish his claim to pre-eminence in worthlessness.

"I've broken every commandment," he moaned, "each one more ingeniously than the last."

"I've had a pretty good shot at most of them myself," I said, anxious, if possible, to align myself at his side without disputing his own distinctive prowess.

"I've committed every sin," he went on, "every sin in the calendar."

I was disposed to observe that sins are not normally listed in calendars, but then it occurred to me that he might belong to some peculiar sect which issued an annual Almanac of Wickedness for the purpose of keeping its adherents on the straight and narrow. I laid my hand on his shoulder, but he withdrew.

"I'm untouchable. I not only committed every sin; I boasted of it."

"You're still boasting of it," I said gently, hoping to ease his despair. But it had the opposite effect.

"I am, I am. That makes it all the worse. I'm still degenerating. I shall go on degenerating."

"I doubt it," I said. "From what you say, you haven't left much room for further developments in that direction."

"That's true. I'm as evil as can be already," he groaned, illogically incapable of resisting the claim. Noting that argument on this level was not likely to be fruitful, I took his arm and led him up the path beyond the machines, determined to get him away from the scene of his discomfiture. But there was no leisurely stroll ahead of us, for the path led us directly to the front entrance of what looked like a large country house, though it had that air of cold drabness which hangs around stately homes that have been adopted for official or institutional use. We were offered a dismal welcome in the entrance hall. "SINNERS ALL," I read aloud. My companion didn't raise his head.

"It's the right place for me," he said, obviously under the unflattering delusion that I was in the habit of dropping my aitches.

A door on the left was distinguished by an even more fascinating notice:

SACKCLOTH AND ASHES supplied here.
Apply within.

My companion suddenly came to life when I read this aloud. For the first time an air of something like active eagerness possessed him and he walked before me through the door.

A depressing-looking gentleman stood at the other side of a counter in what looked like an enormous cloakroom. Into the dark distance behind him stretched rows of hooked frames, laden with long shapeless garments made of sacking. Half a dozen dust-bins lined one wall, painted with the label "ASHES."

"You are both miserable sinners?" queried the attendant, as if questioning our credentials.

"That's right," said Smith, brightening a little.

I merely nodded. The attendant apparently desired something more definite from my lips as well, for he addressed me particularly.

"You too," he said, "are you the lowest of men?"

"The next lowest," I said, hesitantly, fearful of offending my companion.

Obviously Smith found my loyal support encouraging. He nodded vigorously in assent to my modest claim. Clearly he appreciated the restraint which I was exercising on his behalf and he actually allowed the beginnings of a smile to crease his features as he glanced at me in acknowledgment. I knew I had made a friend. The attendant, however, gave me an uncertain look, as if my claim were inadequate and, for one dreadful moment, I wondered whether my impulse of friendly consideration for Smith was going to cost me the right of formal enrollment. But Smith himself came to my rescue.

"I am a special case," he said. "I've broken every commandment, each one more ingeniously than the last."

"I can almost equal that," I said. "I've failed only in ingenuity. I broke them all in the same pedestrian way."

This seemed to satisfy the attendant without offering any serious challenge to Smith, and I felt I had acquitted myself well. At any rate the attendant immediately provided us each with a sackcloth garment, shaped like a loose cassock. Having got inside these, we were each handed a length of coarse string to perform the function of a girdle. To complete our array, the attendant next produced a couple of skullcaps made of the same material as the gowns. He placed these on the counter upside down. Inside each was a pocket which fastened with press-studs. The attendant opened these, produced a grocer's sugar scoop, and shovelled a quantity of ashes from the nearest dust-bin into each pocket. As he refastened the press-studs, Smith showed some disappointment.

"I thought we should be able to smear our faces," he said.

"You will be free to do so, if you wish," said the attendant. This cheered Smith.

"Good," he said.

The attendant raised an admonitory finger.

"But I must warn you of the spiritual dangers of trying to claim special distinction for yourself among the penitents. The wish to be distinguished by outstanding marks of wretchedness may spring from vanity."

"It does, it does," said Smith eagerly. "That's what I meant when I said I was a special case. I'm rotten even in my penitence."

The attendant nodded appreciatively and Smith gave a peculiar grunt of contentment, having thus tortuously achieved one more triumph of self-depreciation. We put on our skull-caps.

"What do we do now?" I asked.

"Go to the Assembly Hall. A penitential procession will set out shortly. You will soon be on your way."

"Where to?" asked Smith.

"To Heaven, of course."

Smith was visibly taken aback. It appeared that journeying to Heaven had formed no part of his programme.

"We're not worthy," he protested.

"Of course not. But if you don't set out, you won't be able to feel the full force of your unworthiness. There is no pain in being unworthy of something which is not in prospect, but beyond your conceivable grasp."

Smith looked bewildered.

"Heaven is surely a place of bliss," he argued.

"It is. And with every step you take toward it, your misery will increase through your growing sense of unworthiness."

This cogently-presented prospect of increasing torment appeared to reconcile Smith to the journey, and we moved off in search of the Assembly Hall. This was not difficult to find, but when we got there it proved to be empty. However, there was a helpful attendant at the door, an old man who had the trained servant's knack of combining familiarity with some degree of deference.

"Just you wait 'ere, sir. They'll be along any moment. They've nearly finished their disciplines."

"Sounds grim," I said jocularly, fishing for information.

"Nothing in it, sir, nothing at all. Just a little matter of ropes. They swing 'em over their necks all right, but it doesn't 'urt. They see to that."

"Couldn't we join them?" asked Smith, obviously interested in this technique of self-punishment.

"Too late, sir; all but finished now. And, between you and me, it's not worth doing anyway. Empty ceremony, that's what it is. But I've seen the day when disciplines *was* disciplines."

"You've been here a long time?" I asked.

"I 'ave, sir." He nodded.

"And seen many changes?"

"I should think I 'ave. The place isn't what it was. Too easy by a long chalk. They call it a penitentiary, but if you ask me, it's nothing but a blooming 'ospital."

"Well, we've got the right clothes," I said.

The attendant was scornful.

"I've seen the day when you'd both 'ave 'ad your

'eads shaved. There was no pockets for the hashes then. They was slapped on and rubbed in."

Smith sighed, and a dreamy, nostalgic look came into his eyes. Knowing his propensities and anxious not to see them encouraged, I tried to counter the old man.

"Not very hygienic," I said.

"Penitence is penitence," he said solemnly, "and 'ygiene is 'ygiene. And there's a world of difference between the two. You don't come 'ere for a rest cure, you comes for penitence; and you ought to get it good and 'ot. Time was when I 'ad a couple of lads knocking nails into pilgrims' sandals. And they knew 'ow to use the ropes in those days. But times 'as changed. No blood; that's the rule now. No blood, they say, 'cos it's morbid. But what I say is—what's penitence if it isn't morbid?"

The old man obviously took to heart the degeneracy of modern penitents. And he could scarcely have found a more sympathetic and responsive auditor than Smith, whose eyes glistened when he heard of the outmoded disciplines.

"Why have they changed so much?" he asked regretfully.

The old man shook his head tragically.

"It's this 'ere modern psychology what's done it. We want converts, they say, not perverts. But 'ow can yer tell a genuine convert from a fake, if a fellow isn't allowed to belt 'is own back? No, the place 'as seen its best days."

At the far end of the hall a line of penitents began to file in through the doorway, their heads bowed and knotted ropes in their hands.

" 'Ere they are; 'anging their 'eads; but take my

word for it, there isn't a bruise on one of 'em. Strip down the lot of 'em and you wouldn't find a scratch."

Smith's disappointment at hearing the attendant's tale of increasing decadence was somewhat mollified by the spectacle of the tragic file of pilgrims.

"Let's go in," he said.

"Aye," said the old man. "You'd better join 'em."

As we left him he added a final ironic sally.

"And mind you don't 'urt yourselves. That'd never do."

11

I joined the group of penitent pilgrims with my eyes
open. I knew there was something absurd about their
one-track concentration on self-immolation. Their
unvarying persistence in dismal self-depreciation was
itself a distortion and amounted to a morbid obsession. On the other hand, I was absolutely determined
not to let slip another opportunity for joining a pilgrim band on their journey to the City. I had firmly
resolved that I should not again allow exaggeration or
caricature to drive me from a body of pilgrims, if
there was anything at all congenial about their attitude. There was no doubt that these people were genuinely disgusted with their earthly selves and knew
the need for self-abasement, and in this attitude I had
good reason to concur. Everything about the penitentiary was of a piece with my experience in seeing the
film of my life. There was always the element of the
farcical and the grotesque, but behind it all lay the
recognition of fundamental truths about personal sinfulness and unworthiness.

So it was that, clad in sackcloth, we marched in single file along the Highway to Heaven, our heads

bowed and a deathlike silence hanging over us. There was an additional comic irony for me in the fact that I had come to this as a result of failing to join the magnificent band of boisterous pseudo-mediaevalists. Moreover, a wry smile curled my lip when I cast my thoughts back to Manuel's warning. This was what I had chosen; the dramatisation of penitence in a dismal file of dressed-up misery.

Being a latecomer, I had managed to secure the position of last in the file. Actually Smith had disputed with me for this position; but he had waived his claim when I pointed out that there might be a discipline in which pilgrims had to beat the backs of those they followed. The mere mention of this unlikely possibility had settled the dispute. Smith was the last man to risk forgoing any torment through acceptance of an advantageous position. So I enjoyed the convenience of being able to look round occasionally without being observed.

It turned out to be very useful that I was able to look behind. For thus I had warning of an event which proved so interesting that few penitent heads remained bowed as it took place. We were approaching the top of a long climb when, incredible as it may seem, we heard behind us the once-familiar noise of a motor vehicle. I turned immediately. It was a car, careening down into the hollow from which we had just toiled upwards, but the momentum gained from the car's rapid descent quickly ran out as it began to climb behind us. Before long it was groaning in bottom gear as it crawled laboriously after us. The noise was considerable. Not only did it groan: it rattled too. And small wonder; for it was a bull-nosed Morris Cowley, dating from the early nineteen-twenties. But my sur-

prise at its appearance and age was quickly swamped
by my astonishment at its occupants. There were five
of them, three being tightly wedged and bolt upright
in the high front seat. These were the Wheeler trio,
Jim driving, Tom portly and bulging in the middle,
and Bert jammed half-hidden against the nearside
door. High and lifted up behind these three, in the
dickey seat, whom should I see but my old friends
Tribulation and Ananias, towering, erect and solemn.
In their high black hats they looked like a couple of
liveried guards at the back of a stagecoach. I wondered what strange accident should have thrown these
five together. As they drew level with us, most of my
companions lifted and turned their heads, and in fact
our procession came to a halt. This proved fortunate,
for the hill was too much for the overladen car, and
Jim must have realised that it would have to shed part
of its load in order to get to the top. At any rate he
stopped, apparently pushing it out of gear and apply-
ing the brake. He ought to have known better. It began to slip.

"It won't hold," he shouted.

Smith and I and two others rushed to the back and
managed to stop it before it gathered speed.

"O.K.," said Jim. "Let it go back gently. I'll steer it
into the hedge."

This manoeuvre accomplished, Jim and Bert
climbed out.

"Wherever did you get this?" I asked.

"Found it," said Tom.

"Just hanging about," said Jim. "No one wanted it.
Hadn't been used for ages."

"No one could make it work," said Tom.

"Until we came along," Jim added.

"And these gentlemen?" I indicated Tribulation and Ananias.

"They missed the bus," said Jim.

"Through trying to save us," Bert explained.

"Gave us the works," said Tom. "A real bellyful. Blood and thunder and merry hell."

"And when they got back to their tent the saints had departed."

"It puts us under an obligation," said Bert. "We felt we ought to do something."

"Tried to charter a plane," said Tom, "but had to make do with this."

"Nearest thing they'd got," said Jim. "But we'll make it. They can't be far ahead of us now. They may be saints, but they haven't got wings."

Tribulation and Ananias still sat motionless and upright in their dickey seat.

"Come down, O Israel!" said Jim.

The two sombre figures rose from their perch simultaneously and clung to each other precariously for support.

"Both the chariot and the horse are fallen," said Tribulation.

"But we are risen and stand upright," said Ananias, visibly tottering.

"Only just," said Jim. "You'd better get down before you fall too."

They alighted. Tribulation gravely shook his head.

"Some put their trust in chariots and some in horses."

"It may be ancient," said Jim, "but it's a damned sight more advanced than a chariot."

"I will open my mouth..." Ananias began, but he was interrupted by Jim.

"You'd much better put your shoulders to the wheel, if you really want to catch those fellows up."

The engine had stalled. It appeared that the mechanical trio preferred the labour of pushing up the rest of the hill to the labour of winding.

"Give it a heave. All together!" Tom urged from the comfort of the front seat. And indeed the work suited the physiques of the others better than it suited his.

Slowly the thing began to move. The sweat dripped from Tribulation's brow and he panted.

"Why hop ye so, ye high hills?" he spluttered. And certainly the gradient was at its worst here.

"Surely you can try winding," I suggested.

"O.K.," said Jim, producing a handle from underneath the driving seat. Bert meanwhile opened the bonnet and prodded the carburetor.

"The Lord shall look upon it," said Ananias, "and, behold, it shall be driven away."

"A perfect combination," said Jim, inserting the handle. "They've got the faith, and we understand the works."

His efforts were successful. The engine roared into action. Jim leaped into the driving seat and was heading up the hill in no time.

"I'll wait for you at the top," he shouted.

The top was not far off, so that was no great hardship for anyone. In fact Tribulation and Ananias seemed only too glad to be on their feet and able to stretch their legs. They strode vigorously to the top. There, however, they paused hesitantly before the car. In spite of their earnest desire to overtake their companions, they were not eager to return to their uncomfortable perch. The sight of the open dickey seat and its hard unupholstered bench once more moved them to an expression of their feelings.

"The Lord hath prepared a seat for us," said Tribulation and he grimly clambered up. Ananias followed him with a groan and sat down gingerly in obvious discomfort.

"He hath set me up upon a rock of stone," he said.

"I am sore pressed," Tribulation continued, while Ananias closed his eyes pathetically.

"Like as the heart desireth the waterbrooks," he said, "I long for the healing touch of gentle springs."

Jim tugged and Bert pushed at the bulk of Tom in order to make room for another.

"In and out," Tom panted, somewhat ungratefully, since he had never stirred from his seat. "Might as well walk. No guts in the thing. What can you expect from eight horse power?"

"He hath no pleasure in the strength of a horse," said Tribulation gloomily.

Jim waved his hand.

"For pete's sake, cheer up. The thing's right enough. It'll get us there. Look at these poor blighters, padding along like so many sacks of spuds tied up with string."

"Gives a chap the creeps to see them," said Tom.

Smith sprang to the defence of our penitent band.

"The road to Heaven is hard."

"I'll say it is," said Tom, "and strewn with precious bleeding stones."

By this time Bert had managed to squeeze himself in at Tom's side and, with my assistance, the door had been jammed shut so as to contain them all.

"You left Miles behind," I remarked, as they prepared to leave.

"Miles behind," repeated Tom, shaking at his own joke.

"He was a bore," said Jim. "Didn't know a big end from a rolling pin."

"Quite true," Bert explained. "He thought a plug was something to keep the water in the radiator."

Jim revved up the engine.

"All set?" he called, "We're going to start."

Tribulation stiffened himself.

"I will thank the Lord for giving me warning," he said.

Ananias gripped the body of the car and his features assumed the fixity of martyrdom.

"This also shall please the Lord, better than a bullock which hath horns and hoofs."

"Away we go!" Jim shouted, and the car lurched forward. Within a few moments it was lost to sight.

Our dismal procession moved on again, and I was less at ease than ever. The strange encounter had made me think hard. I thought I saw a meaning in the odd liaison between the evangelicals and the Three Wheelers—a meaning which had been unwittingly summed up by Jim in his wisecrack about faith and works. The motorminded trio had indeed something to offer, and they were offering it. Their practical capacities had enabled them to come to the rescue of Tribulation and Ananias. Moreover these latter two had qualities of conscious piety and zeal which the practical trio had never developed in themselves. The coming together of the two groups was thus peculiarly happy and significant. By a sharing of resources the five of them were heading for the City. Two provided the motive and purpose; three provided the means. It is a parable, I thought, mentally patting myself on the back for having discovered it, and what a fortunate chance it was that had produced it!

A moment later I was aghast at my own stupidity.

Why should I call such an event a "chance"? The concept *chance* was based on an utterly negative notion. It connoted mere lack of purpose. Who was I to say that there was no purpose in this coming together of five people for journeying to the City? To describe the event as a "chance" was to question God's providence and omnipotence. Surely the Divine Providence was at work here. Surely the strange progress in the old car was part of a pattern worked out under the eye of God Himself. The two groups were meant to come together thus, for their mutual benefit and their joint salvation.

Logic is a disturbing instrument with which to explore the realms of the spirit. No sooner had I pounced upon this truth than its inevitable corollary stared me plainly in the face. If their coming together was under the guidance of Providence, what of my union with the penitent pilgrims? Was this what God meant for me? Was this another working out of His Will, or was it a rebellion? I could scarcely bear to face the question, for the encounter with Jim and company had left me feeling completely hypocritical in my present guise. Amid all the possible fashions of self-transcendence which journeying pilgrims assumed, I had chosen the most strident guise of self-professed piety. I had dressed myself up in such a way that my whole appearance was a concrete claim to humility. At every step I was shouting to the world—Look at me; I'm humble, penitent, unworthy, self-abased! I was a walking challenge to the consciences of others, involved in carrying a pharisaical claim to humility right up to the Gates of Heaven.

The Three Wheelers had gone their way, boisterous and preoccupied. The freshness of their banter itself expressed an unselfconscious lightness of heart; whilst I was a walking caricature of pious misery. If I was right, then they were wrong. But they weren't wrong. How could they be? They were engaged in helping towards Heaven two men who had tried to help *them* towards Heaven. The important thing in their eyes was the getting there. But our hearts were set on something else. The very appearance of our band proclaimed that something else was of prime importance—the outward show of organised contrition.

Fool and hypocrite that I was, I had seen the dangers of every form of self-transfiguration except the one I had adopted. I had criticised the dramatisation of chivalry and courtesy, sportsmanship and self-control, scriptural faith and prophetic zeal. And, having criticised, I had chosen to dramatise the one utterly undramatisable reality of self-surrender in humility and contrition. I might have joined in transfiguring earthly worship, earthly zeal or earthly striving. Instead I had tried to transfigure the one utterly untransfigurable inwardness of earthly self-denial.

I checked myself in this train of thought. For surely self-denial *could* be transfigured? It could. But not by parading itself in fancy dress: for this was itself the negation of self-denial. The means cancelled out the purpose and the end. To parade self-denial was to annihilate self-denial. To dramatise humility was to destroy humility. This was not the proper way to walk to Heaven. It was the appropriate way to walk to Hell.

For the first time a sentence of Manuel's came back to me which I had been oddly reluctant to recall hitherto. "Insofar as you have already chosen Heaven, to that extent you already enjoy Heaven." It would have

been easy to reflect upon that in the company of Annot. Indeed I had begun by enjoying Heaven. But my
progress since that time had been a regress. I had
walked further and further into misery until now I
carried the advertisements of self-chosen gloom upon
me like a man with sandwich boards.

I had chosen the one thing I could not choose—the
self-willed transfiguration of self-denial. There was
only one transfiguration of self-denial, God's sacrifice
on Calvary. Such feeble impulses to self-denial as I
had managed from time to time to serve—I might
justly hope that these would be taken up and involved
in the consummate eternal act of divine self-giving;
that was a proper hope. But to carry before me, as it
were upon a banner, an exaggerated claim to self-
abasement—to carry this before me in order to thrust
it before the eyes of those who kept the Gates of the
Eternal City, this was a mockery and a blasphemy un-
matched even in my earthly record of hypocrisy. It
was the sin against the Holy Ghost.

Suppose all the journeying pilgrims really achieved
self-transcendence after the fashion they adopted on
their pilgrimage. Suppose they all attained eternally
to the realisation of the roles in which they posed
along the road. It had occurred to me that they might.
In that case, our lot would be to spend an eternity of
self-claimed misery and self-advertised piety. Could
we continue, in Heaven, to hand out these public tes-
timonials to the reality of our penitence? I was involved in an unthinkable farce; the only farce I had
witnessed above which was finally and intrinsically
farcical to its very roots.

I had inwardly vowed, on joining this pilgrim body,
not to leave it except for something better: and Providence enabled me to keep my vow. As we filed silently

along the roadside I sighted a distant spire, which soon revealed itself as belonging to a little church. It stood a few yards back from our road on the right-hand side, lifted up above us on a low green hill. An impulse stirred me, and I knew it was a sound one. As our line of bent heads moved past it, I turned from my companions, unobserved, ran up the grassy slope, entered the church through the porch, and knelt down immediately at the back.

"Lord, have mercy upon me," I prayed, "and upon all departed souls," and "grant me, O God, the guidance of Thy Holy Spirit."

They were simple prayers: yet it is among the more astonishingly farcical incongruities of my pilgrimage, that they were the first earnest prayers I had uttered since I had begged for companionship in the far-off Uplands. My prayer then had been answered immediately. Annot had assured me that here all my prayers would be thus answered. This led me to expect something. I waited for a voice from within the City. And, when nothing happened, I repeated my request for guidance the more frequently and fervently.

But the silence all around me remained unbroken. There was no voice, either without or within. Yet the quiet was neither tranquil nor restful. I did not feel that I had reached a place even of temporary harbourage. Perhaps this was because, by its very situation, the building could not give rise to those feelings so often aroused in earthly churches—the sense of having entered a place that has served the spiritual needs of a community through many generations. This place was not designed to be the spiritual home of a residential neighbourhood. It was a place to visit, not to dwell in. It was a shrine to be reverenced and then quickly left behind. Lingering here would never bring peace.

One feature of the church especially strengthened this impression—the unusual rood screen. Most roods have a static quality, quietly summing up the intense finality of the *Consummatum est*. This rood was all movement and incompleteness. It did not bear a central crucifix, but the bowed figure of Our Lord carrying the cross. There were no other figures. In spite of the dignity of the statue and the spiritual impetus which it engendered, I felt there was something theologically inadequate—almost heretical—about it. At the very gateway of the chancel it seemed to suggest that Redemption was not yet achieved. It was wrong, I said to myself, this symbol before the altar of Suffering Love not yet fulfilled in sacrifice. It is wrong, this permanent embodiment of torment not yet intensified into Atonement. It is more than can be endured, this everlasting bearing of the burden of human sin without the consummating act of final Redemption which eternally washes it away. What an appalling image to set before the worshipper; Divinity forever bowed down by the weight of man's shame and guilt! What more desperate situation than to stay forever at the stage of worldwide agony before forgiveness is won.

No sooner had I said this than I knew, confusedly, that I had made a comment about myself. Was not this the error of our penitent band? Was not this what they were trying to do—here beyond the world, before the eternal sanctuary of God, to prolong the enduring of unforgiven guilt? Was it not a blasphemy to climb an everlasting Calvary in unredeemed self-immolation, as though the Blood had never been shed?

Solus ad victimam procedis, Domine.

We are the forgiven sinners, yet we try to assume the role of suffering redeemers. What arrogance it was, this mummery of unnecessary martyrdom on the safe side of the grave. What profanity, this parade of gratuitous self-giving before the House of Him who was from everlasting to everlasting the Giver of all things. What perverse ingratitude, this untimely drama of misery on the threshold of the City of risen light and joy. I squirmed in my hateful clothes, the inescapable symbol of my untempered pride.

"O God," I prayed, "grant me the grace to accept Thy forgiveness. For this is harder for me than to accept my own sinfulness."

Even this prayer seemed inadequate to the magnitude of my blasphemy, and I strained after words to express my shattering self-accusation.

"O God of all Mercy, forgive me my penitence, the last of my blasphemies and the consummation of my pride!"

In the empty silence I looked for some sign as one might open the Bible for counsel at a time of desolation. There was but one verbal message to be seen in the church—the inscription along the base of the rood screen.

Go forth upon thy journey, Christian soul.

It seemed hard to have to go back to the Highway with no guidance more distinct than this; to return to the journeying and questing which had seemed to lead only from desolation to desolation. So I closed my eyes for a final moment of eleventh-hour expectancy and allowed no thought to intrude. Waiting upon God, I heard no word, so I rose to carry out the injunction of the only message the building proclaimed.

I bowed in the direction of the distant altar, lost in

dimness behind the glow of a single central sanctuary lamp, and I turned to leave. My own footsteps on the stone flags were an almost alien presence to me in the utter stillness. My stretched-out shadow contracted itself to nothing as I reached the door. Despondently, I lifted my arm and laid my hand on the latch. But I did not open the door. It was opened for me and, standing before the brightness of Heaven's unbroken day, an impressively upright figure received me from the darkness into the light.

I did not have to be told that it was my own Guardian Angel, Lamiel.

12

For the second time I was walking the Highway to Heaven in the company of a congenial friend who could instruct and advise me. I resolved that I should not lightly throw this advantage away though I was a little apprehensive what Lamiel might say to me. I half-expected a devastating cross-examination. On the other hand, I experienced in his presence a new sense of security, which threw into relief the various tensions I had recently undergone. I looked back on my pilgrimage hitherto, seeking the clue which would unite my disjointed experiences in a tidy and significant pattern; but only the faintest outlines of a pattern were as yet discernible. I had embarked, with Annot, on a journey full of hope and promise. I had dissipated the hope and trampled on the promise in a series of curious and undisciplined deviations. And now, in a more chastened mood, something of the early hope and promise returned to me. I trusted that the detailed shape of the whole progress might now be made clear to me, and I hinted to Lamiel that I was searching for the meaning of things.

"I feel as though I have been disciplined," I said.

He smiled and glanced at my sackcloth.

"You certainly *look* as though you have been disciplined."

There was shame for me in this.

"Yes," I said. "I ought not to be wearing these. I can see now that they are the wrong clothes."

"Why are they wrong?"

I faltered over a difficult and subtle train of thought.

"Because they establish a claim which I have no right to make. They were meant to express penitence; but really they express pride in penitence."

"You think that is why they are wrong?"

Lamiel did not sound convinced.

"Yes. They parade something which cannot be paraded. I ought to have assumed a dress of joyful self-transcendence: then there would have been no danger of making a mockery of self-abasement."

Lamiel shook his head.

"They are not very good reasons," he said.

He spoke gently, yet he withered all my new-found sense of relief and security. With a few words he indicated that the chastened thought, bred of pain and tension, was not after all the illumination it had seemed to be. He saw my distress and continued.

"If the personality is such that it makes a vanity of penitential dress, will it not likewise make a vanity of ceremonial costume?"

"Maybe," I said, "but surely we can safely parade in a joyful ceremony with our heads held high, while it is spiritually perilous to flaunt in sackcloth the claim to humility and self-surrender."

"There is the same danger of flaunting in either case. Either form of dress may be worn with or without vanity and self-display."

"You mean that it isn't what we do that matters, but the inner state of our own souls?"

Lamiel closed his eyes.

"No, no, no. I didn't mean that at all. It's an utterly false antithesis. What you do will be intimately related to the state of your soul. And what you do matters supremely. Can't you see your error? You are thinking all the time about the state of your own soul."

I tried to defend myself.

"I was trying to avoid the dangers of making spiritual claims for myself."

"Exactly. But this obsession with not making spiritual claims is of the nature of a spiritual claim itself. This concern that the soul should not flaunt itself is a self-conscious concern for the soul's unselfconsciousness. Your vanity takes the form of an obsession with your own humility."

"You've tied me into knots," I said. "Now untie me, please."

"We can begin by reversing a perverted earthly epigram. Heaven is not a state of mind: it is a place."

"I understand that."

"So far, on your pilgrimage, you have given little thought to the place you are going to. You have been too busy thinking about yourself."

"I wanted to make myself fit for Heaven, as far as a sinful man can."

"And therefore you concentrated, not on Heaven, but on yourself. You are like a man making a key for a door who fails to take the lock into account. Heaven exists. It is prior to you. Perhaps it contains a station for you. If so, you will have to adapt yourself to that station. It will not adapt itself to you."

"So any preparation is a waste of time?"

"By no means. Preparation of yourself in isolation, without reference to what lies ahead of you; that is useless. But let us take one point at a time. Do you see now why your costume is wrong?"

I hardly dared to trust myself to words and I waited for Lamiel to answer for me.

"It is wrong because it is related merely to your own personal condition: and it ought to be related to the place to which you are going. It is wrong, not because you are you, but because Heaven is Heaven."

"And I have been judging it by reference to my spiritual state."

"Precisely. You asked yourself—What sort of clothes are right for me? It was the wrong question. It should have been—What sort of clothes are right for Heaven?"

"Then what it all amounts to is this: that I must think about Heaven and not about myself."

"Yes," Lamiel agreed, "always avoiding the new danger of thinking about yourself thinking about Heaven."

"It's difficult. I know so little about Heaven."

"Perhaps you know even less about yourself."

This was a shrewd blow and I wilted under it. Lamiel went on more encouragingly.

"Come, come, you know well enough that you are more likely to learn about yourself by thinking about Heaven than by thinking about your own soul. And if you know little about Heaven, that is not because there is little to be known. It's because you haven't taken the trouble to get to know it."

I began to feel very ashamed and awaited some further laying bare of my spiritual emptiness, but Lamiel laid his hand on my shoulder and his tone of voice had a warm and comforting ring.

"It is not entirely your fault. Your mind was not often directed into the right channels by those who instructed you. God alone knows why the Church in your generation should be so silent about the Kingdom to whose Gates she holds the keys. It was not always thus. You have your Scriptures. They are not silent about the glory that awaits you."

"Crowns and shining raiment and crystal seas," I said. "The metaphors have—almost always—left me cold."

"Because you never gave them the intellectual attention which you were eager to give the symbols and metaphors of less inspired poets. There is much in these images to be marked, learned and inwardly digested. For instance, had you pondered and heeded them, they might have taught you not to dress up for a mass demonstration of penitential gloom."

"Except in so far as they stirred feelings of unworthiness." I was still clinging to some vestiges of rightness in this role.

"There is a point at which feelings of unworthiness must pass over into feelings of grateful joy. No man can go on saying 'I am not worthy' once God has said to him, 'I have made you worthy.' For after that point the protest becomes blasphemy. You are not allowed to dispute God's ability to make you, even you, worthy of His Kingdom. The time will come when you are asked to rejoice in the creature He has made you. You will then be wholly of His making, and your joy will be joy in His love and bounty. You will know that you have contributed nothing."

"So we do not make our own Heaven or our own Hell?"

"By the Throne of Mercy itself, you do not. Heaven is wholly and utterly of God's own making. But you make your own Hell. Hell is just that; what you make for yourself. And if you try to make an eternally unworthy sinner of the creature God has freely forgiven and bountifully invited to His own table, you try to make a corner of Hell in Heaven itself."

"Is that what my penitent companions are doing?"

"It is what they are in danger of doing. But their ignorance will be enlightened, as yours is being enlightened. Tell me," he added, abruptly changing the course of his remarks, "what is wrong with your friends who live in Glenville?"

"They don't seem to believe in sin," I said.

"They are rejecting penitence. That is wicked and presumptuous."

"The pilgrims from the Valley of Desolation are not in that situation," I said. "They have accepted penitence."

"They are rejecting forgiveness. That too is wicked and presumptuous."

"But it is a stage nearer the Throne."

"You may as well be hung for a sheep as a lamb. 'He who is not with Me is against Me.' "

For the first time I felt I really understood the meaning of my sojourns in Glenville and in the Valley of Desolation. A sentence from a forgotten sermon came back to me. "When you have accepted penitence, then comes the much more difficult task of accepting forgiveness."

"It's hard," I said, "to accept forgiveness."

"Fallen man finds it much more attractive to picture himself as the conqueror of evil than as the beneficiary of the Victor. In moments of high moral endeavour he tends to cast himself for the role of hero in the fight against wickedness. Of course he is right up to a point. There is indeed a battle to be fought by every man. But the moment of true victory is the moment of realising—fully realising—that the battle has already been won."

"You almost make it sound as though the men of greatest moral persistence are the furthest from salvation."

"Sometimes it is true that they are. You will admit that there is some presumption in the claim to be fighting a battle which has already been won."

"It's not merely presumptuous," I said, "it's ludicrous."

"All pride is ultimately ludicrous. And the pride of self-centred moral piety is, of course, the most ludicrous of all. But I doubt whether you realise how subtly this pride can invade even the understanding Christian soul. Do you not too easily imagine that your Christian occupation is to redeem the world?"

I nodded.

"That is the first blasphemy against Redemption: to behave as though it had never been accomplished. And there is a second blasphemy against Redemption: to doubt its efficacy for yourself or for others. This is to question God's power, His promise and His love."

"Surely," I said, "you cannot mean that a man ought to be convinced of his own personal salvation?"

"As soon as a man begins to picture himself in the role of the saved one, he is thinking about himself and not about his Saviour. That is why, as I said before, there should be more talk among you on earth about the Kingdom of Heaven, and less about your individual spiritual development."

We seemed to be arguing in a circle, and I repeated my former protest.

"It is so difficult on earth to speak of Heaven. Even here one can scarcely think of it except as that from which one is still excluded. It's a walled citadel of mystery: the mind stops short with the image of unentered gates."

"That is not the way to think of Heaven. The world of nature is alive with reflections of its splendours. In every year of your earthly life you pursued them and they eluded you. Life within the Kingdom is the end of all eluding and the end of all pursuit. When you first fell in love, when you first saw the Western Highlands, when you first heard the Beethoven symphonies, did you not then glimpse some infinite fulfilment beyond the grasp of all your mortal strivings?"

"Yes," I said, "but I didn't connect dreams of that kind with going to church and being saved."

"There is no severance, no final discontinuity between the world of Nature and the Kingdom of Heaven. The light of the Kingdom permeates the body of Nature and shines through the fabric of human culture. The voice of the Kingdom speaks to you through your senses and your emotions. All earthly life is astir with the promise of what shall be hereafter. You cannot speak of love and joy, beauty and peace, but you speak of the Kingdom. The tragedy is that men speak unwittingly of the Kingdom and, in their religious teaching, divorce the disciplines of the soul from the blessedness to which they lead. The redeeming of man is not alone the cleansing of sin: it is the transfiguring of all earthly good into the everlasting reality of which it is the manifestation and the lure."

"Then we need below more talk of Heaven?"

"More talk of Heaven and more talk of Hell. Your earth is pitched between the two, and you cannot make sense of it without reference to both. You might as well try to locate a point without reference to its axes, as to understand your earth without thought of Heaven or Hell. You can speak of Heaven in terms of earth's richest promises and potentialities realised and fulfilled, and her highest delights rendered permanent and immutable. You can speak of Hell in terms of earth's frustrations and deprivations forever fettered upon the soul of despairing man. Those are the extremes; and they are personal alternatives for every human creature born into time. Have Christian men become so dead that they can read and hear the promise of love, joy and peace, and not glimpse what these words may mean in terms of personal rapture and enrichment? The glories of God's eternal Kingdom lie before you. Do you men need to be told what unspeakable delight that is—you who have seen sunsets and tasted wine, who have loved wives and reared children, you who have closed your eyes before the poetry of music, and bowed your heads before the music of poetry?"

"For all these analogies," I said, "the blessedness remains inconceivable."

"Of course it does. I don't blame you for not being able to think adequately of Heaven. But you haven't been trying to think even inadequately of it. You've been thinking about your own soul instead. To think about your own soul is temptation. And to possess your own soul is damnation. For your soul, insofar as it is your own, is Hell. Insofar as it is God's, it knows Heaven already. But you must not think that all the machinery of earthly delight, by which God lures the soul of man, itself constitutes Heaven. It does not. In itself it constitutes nothing. As the vehicle of Divine Revelation, it is the means of enriching man's vision of the Kingdom. As an end pursued for its own sake, it is the means of damnation. In the soul's final and irrevocable acceptance of God, all earthly goods are transfigured and subsumed into the reality of joy which is His Kingdom."

"Then it is better for me to think about anything—a tree, for instance—than to think about my own soul?"

"Yes, if you see the tree as God's and the soul as your own. But you ought to know your soul as God's too. And in that case, you won't think about it. You'll be thinking about God."

As I reflected on this, I realised that a part at least of my pilgrimage was taking on a fuller meaning. Hoping that the full pattern of my journey hitherto might yet be revealed to me, I spoke of this to Lamiel.

"I can see now why I was so happy when I first came to the Border Country. I had something—and someone—to think about."

"As is customary, you were reminded of invitations to happiness encountered during your earthly life. But this reminder was not effective in turning your mind resolutely to the Promised Land. You chose the company of those who reject penitence; and then of those who reject forgiveness."

This was what I most wanted Lamiel to expound, and I pressed him further.

"What will happen to my acquaintances at Glenville?"

"One of two things. Either they will be moved to repentance and seek the shelter of the City. Or they will weary of trying to build a settlement here, where the population is always on the move, and they will seek to establish themselves beyond the Uplands."

"Nearer to Hell?"

"Nearer to Hell."

"I am perplexed by one thing," I went on. "I have met people here who seem no different from those I met long ago on the borders of Hell. Miles, for instance. His opinions are not much different from those I heard in Helicon and Fordshaw."[1]

"No man is saved or damned by his opinions. Deeper than all the talk and intellectual activity, there is an inner directing of the will and a life of the spirit. These things you cannot measure. God alone knows them. But do not be deceived by geographical analogies. We are still outside the City. And ultimately all that is not Heaven is Hell. You have had some experience of Hell. I think you know that the only good thing you can do there is to get away from it."

"And the only good thing I can do here is to move on to Heaven?"

Lamiel nodded. I had the opportunity to clear up my last difficulty.

"Then the Pilgrims Trust for processions to the City is a good thing."

"It despatches people on the right journey. It teaches them to dress up in their Sunday best; and that is better than sackcloth and ashes. If offers them hope on the basis of whatever faith there is in them. Of course, those you saw preparing to set out had much

---

[1] Two cities visited by the author in the course of the adventure recorded in *The Devil's Hunting Grounds*.

to learn. Like you, they are now learning it."

Then he suddenly changed the subject.

"Our walk is almost ended. We have spoken about your ill-considered costume. Now it is time to do something about it."

"Nothing is simpler," I said. "I am well attired underneath."

We both stopped, and Lamiel dragged the sackcloth over my head. Then he folded it neatly.

"It is the old man," he said solemnly. "Have you a match?"

I had.

"It has been with you for a long time; too long. It was born in your childhood. You will have forgotten that."

"I can place the date of birth exactly," I said gleefully. "It was at a certain Christmas party when I was six."

Lamiel smiled.

"Ah yes. They are nothing if not scientific in the House of Remorse. You cannot catch them out on facts. But they are weak on interpretation. Your cap, please."

He laid the gown on the grass at the roadside and placed the cap on top.

"The very fabric of the self you claimed to be. The thing which was you in splendid isolation from the Will of God. The very frame of your once-born, unregenerate self."

He struck the match and set fire to the garments.

"It was always destined for the bonfire," he went on. "The crucial question was whether or not you would be inside it when it burnt. Fortunately, you aren't. You're on the right side of the flames."

Lamiel's wry humour could not conceal his inner gravity and the little ceremony filled me with awe.

"It was a near thing," I said.

"Very near. You had dressed up for the firework display and were on the point of setting out. But at the eleventh hour you remembered a previous engagement. A little matter of an invitation to a Wedding. The Bridegroom got in first. So the old Adam had to go alone. And he's finding it hotter than he bargained for."

"It smells," I said, withdrawing a little, as the flames became thick smoke. Lamiel kicked the black embers.

"Dust to dust," he said, "and ashes to ashes. They have made their progress from the dust-bin to the earth. For a little while they decked out a stubborn soul."

"Now they are nothing."

"Now," he said, "they are only a black mark on the road to Heaven."

13

My crossing of the Border Country ended for me as it had begun—on the edge of a cliff. But there were no further similarities. I stood at Lamiel's side, looking down upon a seashore, and the vast expanse of smooth sands was as full of life as a holiday resort in summer. At first sight it seemed as though everyone I had seen at the Pilgrims Trust encampment was before me again. Certainly it was easy to distinguish the mediaevalists in their colourful costumes and the sombre, black-suited evangelicals. The frock-coats and the sporty men and women were there too, looking not the least out of place amid the astonishing variety of dress and equipment. This variety had an additional enrichment in that everywhere angels mingled with the crowds. Soon it became clear that this was something more than a confused throng of people, for the moving masses grouped themselves and, with Lamiel's assistance, I was able to appreciate the orderliness of the scene.

The focus of everything was a ship that stood some way out to sea. It had the appearance of a ferry. In the body of the vessel, between high decks on the port and starboard sides, a lower platformlike deck of immense proportions looked almost as though it were designed especially for transporting motor vehicles; but its purpose was far different, as I soon realised. A central block of cabins bridged it with a magnificent sweep, like the arch spanning some enormous chasm in mountainous country. From the ship's mast floated a flag inscribed with the *chi-ro*. Lying still, couched like a living creature at rest upon the sparkling water, this vessel immediately stirred at one and the same time all the longing that we call wanderlust and all the yearning that we call homesickness. This fact alone revealed her purpose and her destination.

"She carries us on our last voyage," I said.

"*The Ark*," said Lamiel. "The Ark of the New Covenant. You will find your peace in her and through her."

"I can't think how she manages to look so beautiful, hollowed out like that. Somehow it doesn't spoil her lines; it improves them. I suppose there's some purpose in her shape."

"She takes you to her heart, if she takes you at all. She is your shelter and your Mother, and she sails under the guidance of the Star of the Sea."

I was beginning to understand.

"She has an altar?" I asked.

"At the east end of the vast middle deck. You will worship at it on your voyage."

I became intensely interested in the organisation now emerging among the crowds below. It seemed to be the work of that small band of mediaevalists who were mounted on horseback. They cantered to and fro along the edge of the tide, issuing instructions and picking out groups and individuals for special duties.

Soon the vested clergy, acolytes and thurifers had formed themselves into a huge semi-circle facing the Ark, the mitred bishop in the centre. The censers swung together and clouds of incense rose from the extreme ends of the arc. Obviously the candles were now protected by glass shields, for they continued to burn in spite of the fresh breeze. Behind this splendid curve, surpliced singers, uniformed "deaconesses" and members of orders in religious habit formed themselves into a choir, and behind these in turn the bandsmen assembled in a block.

Before this delightful gathering of mixed liturgical splendour lay a boat about the size of a lifeboat. A number of the men in sports dress and of the women in gym-slips and eurhythmics costume had taken off their footwear and, wading out, they drew in the boat's anchor and together held her still. It was plain that she was going to be used to transport pilgrims to the Ark. As they held her, the rowing Blues, bearing their coloured oars, waded out, and the eight of them took their places on either side. I remarked on them to Lamiel.

"Their training was more useful than I imagined."

"There is no good thing that cannot be used. I will tell you something else which it may be good for you to know. One of them is a Carcastrian."

"I don't think I ever thought it utterly impossible for a Carcastrian to be saved. God's mercy is inexhaustible."

Lamiel smiled and added,

"And His ingenuity past finding out. Even unlikelier disciplines than that have their uses."

He drew my attention to the activities of the Three Wheelers. A small number of pilgrims, older and less agile than most, still stood in a little group on the top of our cliff not far from ourselves. The rough track down to the shore had daunted them. The Three Wheelers were making a series of journeys in their ancient car up this formidable track and were transporting the weaker brethren down to the shore, one at a time.

"They keep their interest to the end," I said.

"Not quite to the end," Lamiel corrected. "When they board the Ark themselves, I'm afraid they will have to leave their car behind."

"Will it hurt them?"

"They will have other things to think about."

The immediate purpose of the organisation below now made itself clear. The mounted horsemen picked out pilgrims in turn and, one at a time, they came to kneel before the bishop and he made the sign of the cross over them.

"He is blessing them?"

"And absolving them," Lamiel added. "The last absolution and the last benediction in the Church Expectant."

As each pilgrim left the presence, he rose, genuflected and then turned towards the Ark and walked down to the sea. The wading athletes carried each one above the water into the boat, and soon the first load was being rowed out over the blue water to the waiting Ark.

Then came the music, more difficult to describe than anything I encountered in this concord of indescribable revelations. I knew it; and yet it was more than I knew. I recognised immediately the opening bars of the *Rex tremendae* from Verdi's *Requiem*. Yet the thing soon surpassed all previous experience. Once

I should have described the magnificent *Salva me* as perfect. But its perfections had been enriched. Punctuated by thundering rhythmic repetitions of *Salva me* and *Rex tremendae majestatis*, the yearning melodic surge of *Salva me, fons pietatis* rose in a sequence of modulations richer and more extensive than Verdi's grasp, sure and searching as it is, had reached. The rising cry rang through key after key, climbing endlessly upwards as the boat swept steadily out towards the shelter of the *chi-ro*. And then, as the Ark was reached and the pilgrims climbed out on to the great nave of a deck, the climax of this musical sequence came in a full-drawn-out splendour which I shall never forget. The bountiful changes of key, more abundant than the most exotic harmonies of Wagner, suddenly levelled themselves out into the plain grandeur of the C major cadence which is Verdi's own ending. I could no longer keep silent, and I knew, as I joined in, that every voice on the shore below was also playing its part in the last mighty acclamation, no longer a cry of yearning, however rich, but a great shout of triumph, proclaiming as an accomplished consummation that which it expressed in words of beseeching prayer:

Salva me, fons pietatis!

The music ceased and the boat returned to the shore. Once more, selected pilgrims began to make their homage at the bishop's feet and to wait their turns on the edge of the sea. Lamiel turned to me as if awaiting some further questions, yet not, I felt, as if inviting them, and I was silent. At length he said, "You have nothing more to ask?"

"It is no virtue in me," I said, "but, God knows, I want nothing except to take my turn and be aboard."

"Let us go down then."

We moved along the cliff to the head of the track which led to the shore. Here Jim and Bert were helping an old woman into the car, in preparation for another descent to the sands.

"I've caught you up," I said in greeting.

Jim shook his head in mock ruefulness.

"You can never tell with these religious chaps. I thought we were heading for the Keswick Convention, and we seem to have landed at Margate."

"Once you die," said Bert, "you don't know what you're in for."

"You are doing a useful job," Lamiel said.

Jim sighed.

"It's a good thing there are not many more up top here. She's on her last legs, and it's terrible hard underfoot. I've had enough."

"So have I," echoed Bert. "Though it doesn't seem to be much in my line, I shan't be sorry to be singing *Holy, Holy, Holy* and crossing the crystal sea."

"You're all going over?" I asked.

"With Obadiah and Perseverance," Bert said.

I knew what to call them at last.

"And a couple of archangels thrown in," Jim added, "whose names I forgot to ask."

"They were so informal," said Bert. "No introduction and no visiting cards. But they nailed us all right."

"The great pity is," said Jim, "that I can't let the wife know. She probably thinks I'm frying in Hell. And here we are, just off for a cruise with the Cherubim and Seraphim."

"I don't think they are personally represented

among either the passengers or the crew," said Lamiel genially, but Jim only rubbed his hands and continued.

"To think of it. In two jiffs I shall be joining the queue for Noah's Ark."

"Not Noah's," said Lamiel. "That particular model is obsolete."

"It's thundering good luck," Jim went on, "and I've never struck anything like it before. Once or twice I had a bit of a break with the week-end Pools. But what's that compared to a free pass over Jordan and all found?"

"We owe a lot to Perseverance and Obadiah," said Bert. "It's not much we did for them, but they wouldn't hear of leaving us behind. Said they wouldn't go on without us."

"Being a couple of saints," Jim explained, "and well in with the Powers that Be, they found a pair of archangels waiting for them with complimentary tickets. But they wouldn't go off without us. They put the high-ups on to us. Argued with them about faith and works. Told them we were prodigal sons."

"Tom's weight did it," Bert interposed. "They spotted his fatted calves."

"And did those angels lay into us," Jim went on. "I don't know much about faith, but they certainly gave us the works. Made us repeat the catechism, my godfathers they did. Wanted to know who gave us this and who gave us that. And the long and short of it is, that we're booked for blessed peace in the Ark of the Government."

"Covenant," said Lamiel.

"There was a little matter of putting on the new man," said Bert, "and getting rid of the old one."

"That's right," said Jim. "We buried the root of all evil in the shape of three greasy overalls. And now we're all set for the New Jerusalem, where we shall hunger no more and (he sighed) thirst no more."

"I can assure you," said Lamiel sympathetically, "that there is no cause for gloom on that score. The City is not teetotal."

"I felt sure it couldn't be," said Bert. "A dry eternity is unthinkable."

"Quite so," said Lamiel. "You can lift up your hearts."

"Not having anything else to lift up," said Jim, "we'd better."

"Meanwhile there are still one or two people to lift down the cliff," said Lamiel.

Jim clambered into the driving seat at the side of his passenger, and Bert leaped into the dickey.

"All aboard for the land of Canaan," Jim exclaimed. "First stop the Red Sea!"

And they shuddered into motion down the hazardous track.

We followed at a steadier and more dignified pace. As we reached the shore, the boat was plying back from the Ark again. How many journeys it had made I could not guess, but a slight thinning out of the concourse on the beach began to be noticeable. Moving among the pilgrims who remained, I felt a little self-conscious at belonging to the very small minority wearing ordinary everyday twentieth-century clothes. I remarked on this to Lamiel.

"I feel like a member of the Modern Churchman's Union," I said, "which is vastly uncomfortable."

"So it ought to be," said Lamiel. "Modernism is not a thing to speak of here, even in jest. We know what a man means when he claims to be a Catholic or an Evangelical. These terms have meaning in reference to the very foundations of the Faith. But to claim to be a modernist is meaningless here. There is no time to be modern in."

"Is it more meaningless than on earth?"

"Slightly. On earth the claim does at least amount to an admission of slavery to the Zeitgeist—one of the most abysmal servitudes that possesses fallen man. To make the negations of ephemeral fashion a criterion of judgment upon the unchanging Faith is always stupid and almost always wicked. It is a deviation which strains our patience to the utmost. Let us talk of pleasanter things, please."

I knew better than to pursue further a subject so obviously distasteful to my guardian, and we moved in silence towards the great semi-circle of vested priests and servers. I hoped that I might gather more clearly what happened as each pilgrim knelt before the bishop. But it was quite impossible to hear anything of the little ceremony. For one thing, we were not near enough. For another thing, the attendant priests and people kept up a constant litany of prayer as the individual pilgrims were received and absolved. This litany was recited in a low, half-singing tone. In the open air, the chant rose and fell with the movement of the breeze. This lent a strange mystic quality to the incantation which, solemnly recited over souls preparing to set out for the Eternal City, was almost as moving in its simplicity as the triumphant burst of choral music which sent each boat-load on its way.

V: *Heal my soul, O Lord, for I have sinned against Thee.*

R: *Lord, be gracious unto Thy Servant.*

V: *Wilt Thou not turn again and quicken us, O Lord.*

R: *That Thy people may rejoice in Thee.*

V: *Comfort us again, O Lord, after the time that Thou hast plagued us and for the years wherein we have suffered adversity. O satisfy us with Thy mercy and that soon.*

R: *So shall we rejoice and be glad all the days of our life.*

Lamiel drew me away from the centre of things and we strolled along the sand.

"You must wait your turn patiently."

Another boat-load was ready to set out. It was noticeable that the proportion of angels increased in the gathering left behind.

"You do not accompany us," I said.

"Some of us will. Others will meet you on the far side."

"But there are no angels in the boat."

"We have wings," said Lamiel. "They are not merely ornamental."

"Of course. Stupid of me."

"You still withdraw before such crudities. There is that much modernism in you. I once told you before that you are a child of your time."

"We both flew then," I said, "both together."

"We shall fly together again."

In saying this, slowly and deliberately, Lamiel betrayed a touch of sadness quite foreign to his whole mood during our present encounter. This, and the meaningful words he uttered, stirred my curiosity powerfully, and though I dared not question him further, he left me on this occasion with a slight ache of uncertainty which re-arose in me from time to time

during the journey which followed. It was so out of
place amid the general rejoicing that I did my best to
suppress it, but without complete success. And small
wonder, for these few words formed the first small
hint of a dénouement which was destined to shatter
my hopes in an unspeakable disappointment.

But nothing of this disturbed me deeply as yet. I
only saw how members of our common body, rich in
habit and plain in habit, were blessed with the sign of
Redemption and borne into the very bowels of the Vessel of Salvation. And I knew, by the joy on their faces
as they sailed out to seek the shelter of Her embrace,
that one and all they loved Her with unfailing love. No
doubt they had sought Her on earth with diverse af-
fections and inclinations. Some had warmed to Her
splendour and others had rejoiced more in Her simplicity: some had most admired Her sure steadfastness
as She rode the waves, Her mighty keel plunging
through the fathoms beneath to root Her as firmly as a
rock in the earth: others had preferred to praise the
disciplined generosity of Her spacious hold, by which
Her very heart lay open to all who truly sought Her.
But all had recognised Her as their only refuge in the
journey through time to eternity. All now knew Her
for their Mother and gave Her the service and loyalty
of sons.

"Simple truths strike one haphazardly," I said to Lamiel. "We are sons and daughters of the same Mother
as well as of the same Father. Somehow, on earth,
we've managed to sever the word *brotherhood* from its
roots in common sonship. Here one realises that human brotherhood is only secondary and derivative."

"It always is. You cannot be as brothers except in
united love of your Father and Mother. To try to be so

is rebellion and presumption. Empires and commonwealths have crashed by this foolishness."

We had reached the end of the now thinly scattered groups of waiting pilgrims, and the open sands were before us. At the very moment when we turned to stroll back as we had come, the thunder of approaching hooves shook the ground beneath us. A horseman rode swiftly up to us. He wore the emblazoned tunic of a herald and his studded saddle-cloth glinted in the sunlight. He called me by my name and I bowed in acknowledgment.

"Thank God!" I said, for I was beginning to feel the strain of waiting.

"It is the only right thing to do," Lamiel added.

He placed his left hand on my shoulder and raised his right hand in a blessing.

"God be with you," he said solemnly. "May you know peace!"

I wished soon afterwards that I had left it at that; but I didn't. The melodic lines of Verdi's *Requiem* still flowed exquisitely in the back of my mind, and I added,

"Rest eternal and light perpetual."

Again the unexpected look of sadness in Lamiel's eyes. He shook his head gravely. But he left no time for questioning when he bequeathed me this last inheritance of unease.

"God be with you," he repeated. "Now go!"

And I strode towards my final homage on the shores of that eternal sea.

14

As for our going upon the water, how shall I tell the manner of it? There was music and laughter and dancing, and the quieter delights of getting to know one's brothers and sisters in leisurely conversation. I learned that all the pilgrims had had the blessings of angelic advice and correction before their arrival on the shore. This alone sufficiently accounted for the fact that there was no longer anything to irritate or displease in the intercourse between us. For myself, I tried to meet and talk again with those I had encountered during my journey; Father Thomas and Dr. Stubbs, the evangelical divine, Willoughby and Conway and the frock-coats, Perseverance and Obadiah (who now professed an odd preference for the names *Tribulation* and *Ananias*), Eustace and Leonora and Uncle Wendle, the now cheerful Smith, and of course the ebullient Wheelers. I spoke with them all and with a hundred more. And in all interchanges of laughter and talk we looked one another squarely in the eyes, as on earth it is often so difficult to do.

Then there were those solemnities on the great central deck which stretched the full length of the vessel.

We knelt in a temple whose east end was a prow, before an altar whose reredos was the blue haze shrouding the coast of Heaven. The upper deck and Captain's bridge spanned the middle body of our nave like the central tower of a great cathedral. The narrow port and starboard decks stretched above our nave and chancel like clerestory galleries. And it was on these exalted levels that the angels took their station during our solemnities. As we knelt below, they stood above, poised in perfect stillness, their wings outspread as if for flight. It was moving indeed to sing out the *Gloria in excelsis*, afloat on the waters that wash the shores of the eternal City. It was strong and triumphant beyond all earthly assurance to declare the affirmations of the *Credo* in company with a united body of pilgrims, whose eyes were searching the distance for the first glimpse of the spires of Heaven. And in the hush that fell upon us at the *Incarnatus*, the motion of the Ship was like the beating of Her very heart, whose standard was the *chi-ro* and whose figurehead was a Virgin and Child. But I think the most overwhelming moment of all came with the sudden manifest literalness of the invocation calling us to our first *Sanctus* on the sea:

> *Therefore with Angels and Archangels, and with all the Company of Heaven, we laud and magnify Thy glorious Name....*

My eyes ought to have been covered with my hands. But had they been so, I should not have known that the angels around and above me had covered theirs with their wings.

I should omit a most significant feature of my experience on this voyage, if I did not attempt to put into words an idea that occurred to me time and time again. It swept over me at solemn moments of worship and at lighthearted moments of friendly banter. It seized me during the singing of psalms and during the shaking of hands. It flashed upon me at the raising of an eyebrow and at the turning of a head. It coloured my joy in the breeze and the sky and the moving vessel. It was this. I have lived on earth, I said, and the very feel of earthly life is as familiar to my senses as ever it was. I have been in Purgatory and I have seen Hell; but this, this is what earthly life was truly like.

As like as to itself. The strange phrase came back to me from Shakespeare. And yet it was not quite adequate. I wanted to say: This is more like earthly life than earthly life itself was; and unless I repeat that illogicality emphatically, I shall have failed to give a true account of what I felt. To reproduce that feeling in expression, it is not enough to say: On earth we were always trying to be like this and not quite succeeding; though that indeed goes some way towards expressing the inexpressible after which I clutch. Rather, if I may make another attempt where all attempts must fail, let me say: This, just this, is what we were really doing, thinking, seeing on earth, but we never fully realised what we were about.

If ever I knew the bright goodness and hard reality of what is offered to us in earthly life, it was here and now, when I had passed beyond all temporal delight or pain in its offerings. I said to myself, in a strange gravity of joy: If, by some strange chance, I had to return to life on earth, I should not be able to endure to see a fellow being raise his hand in greeting or turn his head in sorrow, let alone smile and weep. For I should know what he was doing, and the roots stirred by his lightest passion; and the extravagant thoughtlessness of his gesture would sting like the cut of a blade.

I was in just such a ruminative mood when the cry was first raised that the shores of Heaven had been sighted. Everywhere there was movement and excitement, as pilgrims sought vantage points for the first glimpse of our destination. Many climbed on to the upper decks. Others moved forward to the prow. Eyes were strained and hands outstretched in search and expectancy, and a low buzz of conversation expressed our tense and awesome delight. I was on the point of moving forward with the rest, when I was suddenly joined by Lamiel. He laid his hand on my arm to restrain me and the gesture surprised me. Neither of us spoke; but I studied his face. There was no rebuke or displeasure in his eyes, but the stillness and patience of their expression seemed to be in conflict with the prevailing delight and expectancy. I felt again the old discomfort.

"They have sighted land," I said.

He nodded.

"Can I not join them?"

He shook his head.

"No. It is not so intended."

In the pause which followed this unthinkably suggestive denial, a sudden hush fell upon the whole ship, quieting the buzz of reverent excitement which had succeeded the first rush to upper decks and prow. I knew without being told that what had formerly been sighted in the distance by the look-outs had now become visible to the naked eyes of my fellow-voyagers. They were seeing the outlines of the City. And they were silent.

Lamiel and I stood isolated at the west end of the great deck, and not a face was turned in our direction. In spite of my guardian's presence, this was a loneliness such as I had hoped never to taste again. I trembled as I spoke once more.

"Do you mean that I'm not going with them?"

He laid his hands on my shoulders as if to strengthen me against the shock.

"This has been a vision. It must end here."

I did not think of the friends I had to leave or of the City I was not to see. I did not think how all the purging and penitence, the hope and expectation, had led to this moment of denial for me alone, where all other hearts were fixed on their everlasting home. I could not think of anything. In the profound stillness my brain was empty of thought and my heart of feeling. It was like the stroke of death: and the utter paralysis of intellect and emotion saved me from the blasphemy of rebellion. Before I could gather my feelings into a coherent response, Lamiel intervened to keep me safe.

"Before you say anything, remember it is His Will."

"His Will," I repeated blankly, trying to grasp the notion as an anchorage.

"In which alone is your peace," said Lamiel solemnly.

I bowed my head and waited for more.

"I shall take you back," Lamiel said.

We turned and faced westwards. Behind us the pilgrims had begun to sing—Abelard's hymn again, the same that I had heard at the beginning of my pilgrimage.

If words can utter the full heart's story,
Let them declare, who partake in this glory,

How great the Sovereign, His high habitation,
How deep the peace and the soul's exultation.

In some strange ironical way it heartened me. I summoned up a smile.

"You said we should fly together again. I ought to have known."

"No," said Lamiel. "You could not have known. But, now knowing, you can submit."

He took my hand.

"I have no alternative," I said. "I can't gate-crash."

Lamiel laughed.

"You never said a truer word."

Sabbath on Sabbath, for seven days in seven,
Rise up the festal liturgies of Heaven.

The singing voices rose in worship behind us, as we stood poised for flight, the towers of the Eternal City greeting all eyes but ours.

"I'm ready," I said. "After all, I've had some experience of visions before."

"That reminds me," said Lamiel, holding back for a moment. "If you write this up—or rather, when you write this up—don't vulgarise it unnecessarily. You can't be expected to do justice to it in the least. But some crudities might reasonably be foresworn from the outset."

"For instance?" I queried.

"For instance, no nonsense about fictional operations and anaesthetics this time and, please, no cheap mechanical tricks like lifts. They would be even more out of place than ever."

"One has to try every means of making oneself understood," I said in exculpation.

"Just put it down as it happened, and leave it at that," he said. "Of course, some of your readers may get it all wrong again, but you must not mind that. The spirit bloweth where it listeth. Are you ready?"

"Quite ready."

"Then hold on tight. It won't be long."

And, with a sudden bound, we were in flight together again.